Opening message

" The most prevalent thing I've heard in my life is the story of people who are misunderstood. Not realizing that, they don't take time to understand others, either. I hope this book will shed light on the need to stop and understand your fellow man before jumping straight to condemnation."

DAYS PASSED

CHAPTER ONE

"Who decides to go to the library the day after school, Tony?"

"Ralph Waldo Emerson once said, 'There is no knowledge that is not power.' I want to grow up and be a successful businessman just like my dad, Brittany."

"Well I'm just saying the library is not the right way to spend your first day as a high school student. We're going to be freshmen next year, and we have to establish ourselves early if we want to fit in."

"Why do we have to fit in? My dad says that the only way for a man to be successful in this life is to be smart and stay three steps ahead of your competition."

What Tony didn't realize was that in Brittany's world, her parents owned a Fortune 500 company. So for her, all you really needed was an image and smart people you could tell what to do.

Tony disagreed. Yet still Brittany tried to convince him. After all, they were still friends.

"Just come and hang out with me this summer. I'd really love it if my closest friend wouldn't blow me off all summer." Tony, being the clueless sweetheart that he was tried to convince her. "I'm not blowing you off, Brittany."

“Well, hang out with me before we start our freshman year. We might not be able to see each other as much when school starts.”

Tony reluctantly agrees. “Yeah, you're right.” Suddenly, he got excited. “We can go to the fair, hang out at the park, go to Coney Island, it will be great!!”

And they did just that. For a month they were thick as thieves. Their parents couldn't be happier for the two and we're proud that their children had chosen such a great counterpart for a friend.

One day Tony suggested, “Hey, let's go to the summer Shakespeare show tomorrow.”

To which Brittany responded, “Sounds like a date.”

The two shared awkward glances for a while before Tony broke the silence. “Well, technically, it's a play, not a day on the calendar, but whatever you say.”

Brittany laughed and hit him playfully. What neither knew of the other was that they had been falling for each other for quite some time now.

The problem for Tony was that Brittany was the first girl he’d really gotten close to and he’d always been a shy kid. The workings of courtship still eluded him at this age. Brittany, on the other hand, had always been very popular but had never found a guy that she deemed worth her time. Except, of course, her friend Tony.

So, the question for her became whether or not it would ruin their friendship if she asked him to be her boyfriend. All of that would remain hidden in subtext for now.

Then tomorrow came and neither one could wait. Tony asked his parents for a little money so he could get the perfect outfit, to which they agreed.

Brittany dressed herself in front of the mirror for an hour before she settled on an outfit she thought would be great for their outdoor adventure. *Will he like this outfit or this one? How will he feel about this top? Am I too overdressed for this? Okay, I just have to pick one and go. I'm sure he'll like it!*

Needless to say, Brittany was a little nervous about going out with her best friend.

Then the time finally came. Both parties were dropped off by their parents at Central Park and the two went about business as usual, except for one unusual detail. Brittany had brought both of them a picnic and a blanket to enjoy during the play. After they settled in, they talked about their parents, chores, the next school year, etc. until eventually the play began, and oh, what a play it was. Brittany was enamored with the play, infatuated with the classic love story that was Shakespeare's masterpiece.

Meanwhile, Tony was just looking at her beautiful face. He smiled as he watched her dazzle in amazement at the play.

Brittany turned to look at Tony, only to see him staring right back at her. They locked eyes.

"Can I ask you something?" they both said as the play continued in the background.

"What were you going to say?" They mirrored each other once more.

Finally, Tony blurted out, "Will you be my girlfriend?"

The awkward silence that usually follows such a request was not present here.

"Of course, I will!" she said. Then Tony reached into his pocket and pulled out a ring he'd bought with the money he'd gotten for clothes.

"You're looking in that window awfully hard, son."

Tony turned around in shock. "Oh, yes sir, I'm sorry."

"What brings you here?"

Tony proceeded to tell him, "There's this girl who I've been interested in for a long time. We've been friends since we were kids and I was just thinking that I would like whoever she chooses to be with to get her a ring like that."

To which the man said, "Hmmm. That's a story as old as time, kid. Tell me, does she feel the same way about you?"

"No, we're just friends. Plus, I think her parents wouldn't approve of me. I'm not rich. I

don't think they would like someone like me to date their daughter."

"Hmmmm... I see...Well, tell me, would I be wrong in assuming you treat her right and you care very deeply for this girl?" the man asked.

"Of course I do! She's the only friend I've had since elementary school," Tony exclaimed loudly before he knew it. Then he drew back in embarrassment, thinking that the man would laugh at him.

"Why are you embarrassed?"

"You probably think I'm weird and want to laugh at me."

"On the contrary I think the only thing that you're missing is a ring," the man said as he smiled approvingly.

"What? I don't even have money for a ring. All I have is $65 to buy clothes to go to a show with her tonight. Even if I was going to give her that ring, I told you, we're just friends. I wouldn't even know how to ask her out."

The man asked, "What if you did have that ring. Would you ask her out then?"

Tony takes a couple steps back, totally stunned.

"I'll tell you what. I'll go talk to the jeweler. You just wait here, okay?" The man walked into the store and talked to the jeweler for a few minutes before returning to talk to Tony.

"It's your lucky day! He says he's selling that particular ring for $65 today. Give me your $65 and I'll go get it for you."

Tony couldn't believe it, but he reluctantly gave the man his $65 dollars.

A few minutes later, he walked back out with the ring.

"Whoa!!! Thank you, sir! I don't know how I can pay you back for this." "Pay me back with your time and listen to the words of an old man. Don't ever sell yourself short. I can tell you are a good kid with a good head on his shoulders, you remind me of myself when I was your age. In life, you get what you honestly work for. When you put all your heart and soul into something, then you can count on something beautiful to come from it. So, do this old man a favor and ask the girl for her favor and give her that ring, will you?

"The grave is full of souls who are still waiting for someday. Do not be one of them. If you feel in your heart this is something you want, then it is better to live with the memory of an effort than to lament and agonize over past loss due to fear and lethargy."

"What does lethargy mean?" Tony asked.

"Hahaha. In due time, my young friend. But I have lost track of time and need to get back to what I was doing. Until next time, kid."

As the man walked off, Tony called, "Hey, at least tell me your name, sir."

The man said, "Just call me Jericho."

As he walked away, Tony looked at the ring in amazement.

Back at the show, Tony held the ring in his hand.

"It's beautiful! I love it," Brittany exclaimed as she put on the ring.

"So can I take that as a yes? Because it feels like it's about 50/50 right now."

"Shut up, dork," Brittany said as she leaned over onto his shoulder.

"O happy dagger! This is thy sheath; there rust, and let me die," said the actress on the stage.

"That's a major buzzkill," Tony said jokingly.

From there, it was pure bliss. Tony and Brittany spent the entire summer together and their parents couldn't have been happier for them.

The next two weeks were what you would expect for a young couple. They spent all day together and spent all night talking about what they would do the next day. They went to the parks to stroll and hold hands while enjoying each other's company. They went to the batting cages, where Tony embarrassed himself, given that Brittany was more athletic than Tony was. They went to amusement parks at night under the supervision of their parents, of course, but they still shared cotton candy and funnel cakes. Life was going very well.

Then came the day every year in which Brittany's father set aside for vacation.

"I'll see you when we get back, okay?"

"It's okay. I understand. You guys go on vacation every year. It's no big deal. Where is your dad taking you this year?"

The two young lovers stayed up on the phone that night talking about the upcoming trip for Brittany and her family. Tony wasn't as onboard with the idea as he let on, but he did understand her situation. That was the time that her father had carved out to spend with his family, due to his busy work schedule, every summer for a couple of weeks before school started back up.

Anyway, this was usually mother-and-daughter bonding time for Brittany. Regardless of how far away from his company he would get, Brittany's dad could never resist answering a business call. Brittany didn't mind, though. Her mother was a wonder woman. She and Brittany had been very close ever since Brittany could remember. Her mother was a housewife, so it stands to reason most of her time was devoted to her daughter, and Brittany enjoyed every moment. She was a very strong, and patient woman. Brittany's mother was, also, a very intelligent and wise woman.

When Brittany had a problem, she would ask her mother. When she needed to cry, she would go to her mother. When she would see her mother was down, she would always bring her mother ice cream and they'd sit on the couch and watch rented movies. They were by all accounts inseparable.

So for the time being, Tony took solace in the fact that Brittany would be back a few days before school started and then he would be able to spend the entire school with her.

"Hey, Tony, do you want to know something?" Brittany asked.

"Sure."

"I'm really glad we got to spend this summer together. It was the best summer I've ever had. Even though our first moment as a couple was followed by a woman stabbing herself on stage!"

They both laughed at the memory of that night.

"Yeah, I can't say that's how I wanted our first date to go. I always like to think of the ending to that night…it was perfect."

CHAPTER 2

For the next two weeks, Tony spent most of his time in libraries, though he soon realized he wasn't able to focus on his studies quite like he used to. He found himself drifting off and thinking about Brittany most of the time. He wondered how she was doing, if she was thinking about him, if she was enjoying herself, if some other guy was hitting on her and stealing her heart while he wasn't there. He had developed quite the imagination since realizing the feelings he had for his crush were reciprocated with equal desire.

Then he would remember a conversation he'd had with his parents about such matters. All Tony had ever wanted was to be the type of man to deserve Brittany and that her parents would accept.

His father, hand-in-hand with his mother, told him, "Son, the best thing you can do for a great woman is to be a great man. Work hard, provide for her, keep her warm, but above all of these, you must love her. This means brightening up dim days, being by her side when she feels all alone and showing love when hate starts to fill her heart.

"If you can do these things, son, Brittany and her parents will be lucky to have a man like you in their lives."

Then Tony noticed how his parents looked at each other and knew he wanted that same love for him and Brittany. So he vowed to himself that he was going to work hard and grow to be a good man for her. This thought usually refocused him for a couple of hours before he started to drift off again.

The two weeks passed. Brittany was back home and she went straight to Tony's house, only to find all three of the family vehicles were gone and that there were no lights on in the house. She went by for the next three days before school started, but every time she was met by the same view--an empty driveway, and dark home. She was still optimistic for the next day. The next day was the first day of school and there was no way Tony's mom would let him miss the first day of school.

"Maybe he's just at the library cramming for school. He was always a bookworm," she said aloud, laughing to herself.

Then the first day of school came. First period…second period… third period…where was he?

For whatever reason, she wondered if her new beau was avoiding her. Then she overheard two girls whispering and laughing.

"I heard his father got laid off and he had to transfer schools."

What could that be about? she wondered.

She decided to find out. So at lunch, she found the girls and asked them, "Hey, who was the kid who had to transfer because his parents were poor?"

"Oh, you didn't hear? It's that Tony kid who walked around with his nose in his books all day long."

Brittany could not believe her ears. What had happened? Why had it happened to Tony? Why hadn't he told her himself?

For the rest of the day, she was distracted, wondering where Tony was and when she would be able to talk to him again.

"HAHAHA, smart rich kid is slumming it with the common folk, huh? Well you're not rich anymore! Mommy and Daddy can't save you now!" Elsewhere, Tony was having to deal with the hazing that came with being an outsider in that part of the city.

He was special, though, because all the kids had gotten wind that his dad had been laid off and had to sell his home, and he was from a family formerly of means.

"Hey, I'm talking to you! You think you can just walk away, huh? Well, I'll see you at gym, rich kid."

Little did Brittany know she wasn't the only one who was struggling with Tony having to transfer schools. Tony didn't know anything about this school, its teachers or its students. All he knew was if the first five periods were in any way indicative of everyday life at this school, he didn't want to be here for four years. He didn't even want to be here for four more hours.

Gym period didn't change that feeling for the better, either. The kid from earlier found Tony and continued the previous hazing. Only now there were no teachers around, so the hazing turned physical. The kid hit Tony in the back of the head, trying to get a reaction out of him.

"I'm sorry, son. We have to move."

"What do you mean we have to move, Dad? What about school? What about Brittany?" Tony was lost with what his dad was trying to tell him.

"You'll go to another school in the inner city where we'll be living from now on. You'll still be able to talk to Brittany, but the two of you won't be able to see each other as much," his father tried to explain.

"We can't move! She'll be back home in a few days and I have to see her again."

"I'm sorry, son. It's done. There's nothing I can do now." As Tony sat in his room that night, he thought about ways to tell Brittany that he wouldn't be around anymore. He thought of ways he could run away from home and still go to the school with her. He thought of ways he would be able to see her after school. In the end, he realized keeping in touch with Brittany would hurt her, knowing they wouldn't be able to see each other anymore.

He sat in his room that night coming to grips with the fact that he would never see his oldest and closest friend, his girlfriend, anymore.

As he sat at his gym locker while this kid was hitting him in the back of the head, he remembered how much he hated his dad, how much he hated this new school, how much he wished he could go back to last summer, how last summer was a thing of the past.

Then he snapped. He turned around and hit the kid, knocking him back into a wall. Then four more kids jumped in and started their physical hazing in retaliation for what Tony had just done to their friend.

At that moment, another kid jumped into the fray. Only this kid was fighting the other kids. This stranger was on Tony's side, and after a few more seconds of the scuffle, the P.E. teacher came in and broke up the brawl, after which, Tony and this stranger sat at his locker.

"Thanks, man," Tony said.

"It's no biggie. You'd do the same for me, right?" the stranger says.

"I don't even know you."

"The name's Jeremy. Pleasure to make your acquaintance, rich kid."

Like a wolf snarling at a rival hunter coming near its kill, Tony snapped, "Don't call me that! My family isn't rich. Not anymore. My name is Tony."

With playful laughter, Jeremy diffused the situation. “Well, Tony, it looks like you’re in for a rude awakening here. Hey, how about I pal around with you? I’m pretty much a loner here myself since my parents left me.”

And with the most cautious part of his subconscious telling him not to, Tony couldn’t help but to sympathize with Jeremy after what he’d just heard. “Sure, that’s fine by me.”

After that, the two boys got through the rest of the day watching each other’s backs.

Meanwhile at Brittany’s house…

“What do you mean you knew? Why didn’t you tell me?” Brittany was furious with her father.

“Sweetheart I just didn’t know how to tell you. His father got into trouble for embezzlement. They don’t have any hard evidence on the man, but the company decided to let him go to save their image. Chances are, when this plays out, his name will be cleared and Tony will be back in no time, dear.”

“Can I go see him at least and make sure he’s okay?”

Brittany’s father exclaimed, “Absolutely not! Until his father’s name is cleared, you are in no way, shape, or form to affiliate with that boy any longer!”

Brittany started to argue with her father, but she knew he was a stubborn man. His word was absolute and that’s how it had always been. Once he made a decision, there was no changing his mind.

"You are the worst dad ever!" Brittany could not believe what was happening and how unfair it all was. She sat in her room crying about the fact that the only person she trusted at her school was gone for good.

Her mother walked in. "Sweetheart, are you okay?"

"No, Mom. How can I be? Tony is gone and the only reason I can't see him is because of my own dad."

Brittany still couldn't believe her dad would say that to her after the summer the two of them had spent together. In her mind, it was the worst thing her father had ever done and there was no betrayal that could ever surpass this one. Her mother, being the loving mother and best friend to Brittany she had always been, tried her best to explain her husband's position to Brittany and the difficult decision he'd had to make, even though she herself thought that it was an unfair judgement on the part of her husband.

"Baby, he just has to think about our futures. I know your father wouldn't intentionally hurt you, but try to understand the position he is in. For him to keep Tony and his family around after everything that has gone on these past few days would hurt his company's image."

"I DON'T CARE ABOUT HIS STUPID COMPANY!!!" Brittany screamed. "I just don't understand why we can't even be friends anymore. Tony has nothing to do with what his dad did and he's not the one who is being called a criminal!"

For the first time that Brittany could remember, her mother was not on her side, which made the situation worse.

She couldn't believe her mother was taking her father's side. "You two never wanted him around, did you? You were just waiting for a reason to send him away, and Tony's dad getting in trouble gave you what you wanted, didn't it?"

She didn't know what to believe or what to think anymore and nothing her mother was saying was helping her understand why her parents were so insistent on why she couldn't see Tony anymore.

"Honey that's just not true." Her mother was still trying to convince her that neither she nor her father enjoyed Tony's extradition.

"Then what is, Mom?! What's true?"

"The truth is, we love you very much! We loved Tony and his parents. As you grow, you will understand. Sometimes in life, just when you think you've found bliss, it will lead to tragedy.

After a long silence, Brittany hugged her mother. She could not stay mad at her for long. She knew her mother would never mean any ill will towards her.

Her father, on the other hand, was a different story. She didn't know if she could ever truly trust her father again. But for now, she would just have to accept the fact that Tony was gone and there was nothing she could do about it.

CHAPTER 3

As time passed, they both would go on to live separate lives. Brittany became a varsity athlete at her high school, playing basketball and softball. She graduated in the top 10% of her class and due to the affluence of her father, she was expected to do great things. She went on to attend an Ivy League school of her choosing.

She decided not to pursue the life of a college athlete and to focus solely on her studies. She was in line to run her father's company one day and she wanted to make sure she was prepared to step in whenever her father was ready to step down. All of this came at the counsel of her mother.

Brittany never forgot her old friend and she could never bring herself to completely absolve her father for his crimes. Since that night, her goal had been to work her way up and out of her father's shadow, because as much as she had forgiven her father for his transgressions, she'd never again trusted his input on what was best for her life. She had become resentful toward a lot of people to the point where the only person who could calm her down or convince her to give someone a chance was her mother.

Her mother wanted desperately for her daughter to make new friends and date again, hoping this would thaw the cold heart her daughter was developing, but to no avail. Brittany found a problem with everything and everybody. Nothing was good enough for her anymore and her mother knew it. Unfortunately, the damage had been done. As much she tried to get her daughter to learn the lesson of forgiveness and letting go, it just wouldn't take. But what could she do?

Ultimately, she put her faith in her daughter's ability to figure things out. She still knew that deep down, her daughter still had goodness in her heart, but there was no timetable when it came to matters of the heart. As she saw Brittany off to college, she'd treated it as a happy occasion, but she couldn't help but try to break through to her daughter one more time. Brittany knew what her mother was doing and didn't particularly care for it, but out of respect for her best friend, she was never disrespectful to her mother.

"I'm going to miss you so much, Mom. I don't know what life will be like without having you to talk to while I eat ice cream and binge on movies," Brittany said while trying to hold back her tears.

"We can still talk on the phone, sweetheart. I always knew this day would come, but that doesn't make it any easier. I'm going to miss you more than you could ever imagine. I can't remember a time in this house without my daughter sleeping in her bed at night."

"I don't see why I have to go off to a university when one is so close to our home."

"No, no, sweetheart. It's good for a person to get out and experience the world, see new things and meet new people. It's all a part of life. That's one of the things your father and I both agree on wholeheartedly. We met each other in a new town during our college days, you know. Speaking of your father, are you sure you don't want to wait for him so you can say goodbye? He should be off work soon."

"Oh come on, Mom. You know *soon* always turns into *later*. I'll be fine. I'll talk to you both once I make it to school."

"Honey, you know you'll have to forgive your father one day. I just don't want you going through life with a resentful heart."

"MOOOMM."

"I'm telling you, one day you'll look back and wish you could have this time back. That is a horrible feeling."

"I know, Mom, but I've told you, I'm not a child anymore. I'm over it, okay? You don't have to worry about me. I'm happy and I'll be fine."

"Let me tell you something, dear. You can lie to your parents, you can lie to your friends, but you can never lie to your soul. When it feels love, it pulls. And when it feels hate, it pushes. Despite what your words say, you still push your father away, and I just want you to forgive before it's too late."

"I understand what you're saying, but I'm not lying to you. I'm fine. When Dad gets home, tell him I'll call him later and let him know I made it safely."

She didn't want her to worry mother about her. She had honestly forgiven her father on the outside. Deep down, though, she hadn't really paid attention to how estranged her relationship with her father had become.

Her mother could see it, however. She could see her daughter drifting off at the dinner table when her father was talking. In fact, she could see her daughter becoming more and more disinterested in her dad's comings and goings. Maybe she did really think she had forgiven her father.

Sadly, though, if that were the case, that option would be much worse. Knowing you feel hatred is as if you are seeing the monster you having to conquer. Even though you might decide to let it consume you, at least you have a chance. Not knowing the monster exists, on the other hand, even when it's so close to you…well, that is a certain death. As she watched her daughter driving away to go to college, her mother prayed her daughter's eyes would be opened to her reality before it was too late.

Meanwhile, Tony was living the life of a misanthrope for most of his high-school career. He didn't participate in sports, nor did he join any of the clubs his school offered, not that there were many to choose from. Nevertheless, Tony was determined to not grow close to anyone ever again. He spent many of his days in the classroom. Even at lunch and in between periods, the only person he would consistently give the time of day to was Jeremy. He and Jeremy were about as close as they could be, with them both being as different as they were.

Tony's mindset had shifted to his studies and getting into a good school so he could be prepared to get a really good job--all so he would not suffer the same fate as his father. He toiled away diligently and daily to maintain a top GPA to help him to gain scholarship offers, as well. Since, of course, his parents wouldn't be paying for his college.

Jeremy, on the other hand, was satisfied being the class clown. He spent his days mainly tormenting his teachers and his contemporaries for multiple reasons, first and foremost because that's just who he was. Always had been. By the time he was a sophomore in high school, his teachers wouldn't do anything more than send him to the principal's office. Jeremy got some sort of sadistic thrill out of seeing the defeated looks on people's faces when they decided to just let him be. He loved to argue, and he loved to wear down and break the spirit of his superiors, which was the complete opposite of Tony's despondent behavior towards everyone.

The second and probably biggest reason Jeremy acted out so constantly was because he knew he could get away with it. He was, after all friends with the school valedictorian. Why should he be worried about his homework assignments or tests? He always knew that Tony would have his back when it came to helping him with his schoolwork, and he was always right.

When push came to shove, while everyone knew that Tony helped Jeremy with his homework, Jeremy always got a few wrong on purpose so no one could ever prove they'd cheated or that Tony had given him all the answers to the test. As far as he was concerned, he was bulletproof. He could smart off to all of the teachers all day and no one could kick him off of any sports team because he didn't play any, no one could kick him out of any club because he didn't join any and no one could get on him about his grades because he maintained a B+ average. The worst of all these was that no one could threaten to kick him out of school because he would enjoy it.

Besides, with the grades he was making, all the teachers pretty much came to a consensus that since he was making good enough grades to graduate and there was no proof of misdeeds. The best thing they could do for their own mental well-being was to just hurry up and get him graduate and out of the school. Little did Tony know he was sowing seeds for what would become their relationship from then on.

Finally, senior year came, and Tony got the scholarship offers he had hoped for. All his hard work had paid off. Because he was from the inner-city school system, there weren't very many Ivy League schools offering him full scholarships, but he was fine with that. There were plenty of other quality schools in the nation which he could choose from. When he finally decided, he broke the news to his parents, and they couldn't have been prouder.

Just like with Brittany, after graduation and before Tony set off for college, they wanted to have one final talk with their son before sending him out into the real world.

"We're very proud of you, son." Tony's father said.

"Thanks, Dad. I couldn't have gotten here without you guys," Tony responded. His parents knew it was a generic response, but it was nice to hear, nonetheless.

They'd noticed a change in Tony when they'd had to move, as well. He had never been overly ambitious when it came to making friends in the first place, but ever since they'd moved, he had been especially removed. Nothing interested him outside of his studies. He didn't want to go to local events, he never wanted to go play ball and he never wanted to explore. He simply stayed to himself while, for the most part, speaking only to his parents and Jeremy, which didn't remedy the situation one bit.

Tony's parents could see Jeremy might become a toxic friend down the road and feared what might become of their son because of it, but because he was the only person Tony would even give the time of day to, they kept their opinion to themselves. "Thank you son, but this achievement is yours and yours alone. You've worked so hard to get into a good college and your hard work paid off. I just wish we could do more to help you along."

"Stop, Dad. It's okay. I know you and Mom don't have the money. Thankfully, my tuition will be paid for because of my SAT scores and if I can keep up my GPA while I'm in college then the rest of my expenses will be paid, too, so don't sweat it."

Tony really felt that way. He didn't want his parents to worry about him and like his father had said, he'd been working towards that goal since he was a freshman in high school, so as far as Tony was concerned, things had turned better than he could have hoped for under the circumstances.

Nevertheless, his father still felt the shame of letting his family down. He'd always seen himself as the type of man who would be able to support his son and give him a head start in these endeavors, and after everything that had happened with his old job at his former company, all he felt was shame.

"I know you don't want us to worry about you, but we're your parents and we love you, so it's a requirement, okay?"

"I'm so proud of you too, dear. You have no idea how great it feels to see our son to grow up to be such a fine young man," Tony's mother said.

"Thank you, Mom. Like I said I couldn't have possibly gotten to where I am without you two being such great examples to follow."

"Just know we love you and we will miss you and you will always have a home here if you ever need a break from it all." She started to cry.

Tony's father stepped in. "Okay, honey, don't embarrass the boy. Didn't you have something you said you wanted to give him?"

"Yes, that's right!" As Tony's mother ran into the house, Tony's father saw this as an opportunity to have one man-to-man with his son before he left for college.

"Son, I know this might be out of place for me, but I just have to say this because I'm worried about you."

"What is it, Dad?"

"I've noticed that since my sins cost you your relationship with Brittany so long ago, you haven't been the same."

"Dad, it's fine. Really."

"No, it's not. It's all too obvious to me you were hurt by that, and for that, I'm sorry. But I just wanted to tell you that even though I know you're not interested in making any more friends outside of Jeremy, you should."

"Where is all this coming from?"

"One of the secrets no one tells us about the world is that if you're not careful, it's going to fight you and try to tear you apart every chance it gets. If it wasn't for you and your mother, I would have lost my way back then. Having people beside me who I loved and cared about was the only thing that kept me upright and putting one foot in front of the other for a long time. I've seen a lot of things in my day, son. The things that happened to me happen to someone every single day. The only difference from me and the ones who get destroyed by that fight is I have someone in my corner to fight for me and I had someone in my corner to fight for.

When the time comes, and life presents you with that fight, I just don't want you to face that demon alone, son. Now I know you're a big strong man and you don't need any help, but at least think about what I'm saying, okay?"

"Yeah, I'll remember it, Dad, and thanks for the advice. I know you're just trying to look out for what's best for me."

"You will always be my son and I will always love you, Tony."

Then Tony's mother rushed back onto the scene. "Here it is!"

Tony's mother carried in her hands a strange object wrapped in a towel. It was a framed picture of Tony and Brittany the summer before they'd had to move. It was clear to Tony that his mother had snuck in this photo from their driveway when neither Tony nor Brittany were aware.

"Why did you keep this, Mom? I haven't seen Brittany in years. You know that."

"It was the last time I ever saw you with that genuine glow of happiness. I couldn't just throw it away. I kept it because I knew one day I would have an opportunity to give it to you and show you that even though you feel like you're alone, I always want you to remember that feeling you had when you were truly happy. I could never bring myself to say it, but now I think it is the right time. Don't live your life alone, son. When you were with Brittany, you were a completely different person. You could do no wrong and you walked around like you could take on the world. I know we were in part to blame for what happened between you two, and that's something we have to live with, but please, son, don't shut yourself off forever. Find that happiness again."

As much as Tony wanted to tell his mother that he was fine and go through the whole tough guy act he'd tried with his father, he knew after hearing virtually the same thing from both parents that they only meant well, so instead he just hugged them.

"I'm going to miss you guys. Thank you for everything you've done for me. I'll try to be home as soon as I can, okay."

After a long embrace and a few more goodbyes, Tony bid his final farewell before he left and headed off to college.

Both he and Brittany were both off to college in separate states and were truly apart from each other. Unfortunately, this would be a long four years for the both of them. As one would expect, Brittany was welcomed into her college's good graces with open arms. Her father knew the president personally and he'd assured her father that his daughter would be well taken care of. To Brittany's credit, she wasn't like all the other Ivy League students at the university. She did not want her privilege to define her.

So while she attended school, she made sure to focus on her studies so she wouldn't have to worry about people saying she'd made it solely because of her father. She might not have outwardly proclaimed hate for the man, but she still wanted nothing better than to be able to make her name usurp her fathers' whenever he was ready to step down. She focused on her studies before anything else.

She socialized whenever she had a chance. She knew it was good to have friends and she liked being around people and talking to people. The only problem was when people got too close. The moment she felt herself drawing too near someone she would pull away for fear of losing another dear friend. That was, until she met Blake her sophomore year. Blake was an atypical Ivy League student himself, but not in the same fashion as his new sweetheart.

No, Blake's trials came in conjunction with his shy nature. He came from a wealthy family, just as the other kids at the university, but he despised the attention which came with being in the spotlight due to his parents' name and fortune, though his actions never showed it. He played lacrosse on the school's team and was a math tutor in his spare time. His shy nature usually kept him from forming strong friendships with his peers and he wasn't a forceful person. In fact, it was his passive nature which caught Brittany's eye.

The few times she'd seen him, he was in the breakfast bar line in the cafeteria. She'd noticed he would order some strange combination of food, all except for one thing. Every day he asked for a bagel with butter melted on top. Every day, the cafeteria cook would give him a bagel with the butter on the side. She'd always wonder why he didn't tell the cafeteria cooks they weren't giving him what he'd asked for and she could never figure it out. The thing that really caught her attention, though, was that every time he left the bar, he always sat at a table by himself. It perplexed to her that one of the athletes on campus would be so reserved and so averse to added attention and abrasiveness.

Eventually, though, because he was an athlete and he was well-known, people would come and sit with him at his table, but it was obvious these coincidences weren't his doing. It was that underlying behavior which reminded her of a certain person she'd known so long ago. The kind of person who wanted nothing more than to be by himself, even though the people around him were so wrapped up in being social.

After noticing him repeatedly, one day she decided it was best that she just leave him be. She didn't know why a guy in his position had chosen to be so passive, but as far as she was concerned, that was his business.

One day when she'd just left one of her gen. ed. classes and had gone to the computer lab to check on her grades, she found Blake was the math tutor on duty in the lab. She went and sat down at a computer in his proximity and watched him out of her peripheral vision. He looked over at her. She saw his glance but didn't acknowledge the look. Blake just sat and stared.

What Brittany didn't realize was that Blake had noticed her around campus, as well. Sometimes in between classes, he would see her around campus and wonder why she didn't seem to have a particular group of friends she was usually with, like the other girls around campus. This was something which perplexed him. She was someone else on campus who came from a wealthy background with a huge name to live up to and yet she also seemed disinclined to being the social lightning rod she could very easily have been. He always thought with her being as beautiful and smart as she was, that it was only a matter of time before one of the other guys on campus would take her off the market. Every day since he had first laid eyes on her, he thought it was just a matter of time until his premonition would come true.

To his surprise, his premonition never came to pass. Now, the girl he had watched from afar all this time was right in front of his face. He noticed her long hair a mile away. He always stopped and looked up from whatever he was doing if he thought he heard her voice.

Now here she was, sitting right in front of him, and all he could do was stare. He knew how impolite it was, though, so after a few seconds, he went back to what he was doing. After a brief couple of minutes, Brittany turned and look at him. She knew he was the same guy from the cafeteria she'd seen so many times. She couldn't figure out why he was staring at her just a few moments ago, which caused her to stare back.

This guy was a confirmed introvert and for whatever reason, he'd stopped what he was doing to take an interest in someone else who hadn't forced themselves into his presence. She wondered if it could be that he had noticed her around campus, as well.

Then Blake looked up at her again and she quickly averted her gaze back to the computer screen.

"Can I help you with something?" he asked.

Normally, he wouldn't come out and be the first to speak, but seeing as how he was a tutor in a math lab, he could play off his inquiry as just being a part of his job description.

"You aren't having any trouble with the computer are you?" he added.

"No. Thank you, though," Brittany responded.

The fact that he'd acknowledged her sent her back down the train of thought as to why he'd chosen to communicate with her of all people. She didn't want to interrupt his work in case it was just solely to do his job. Neither did she want to seem stuck up and shrewish if it wasn't for the sake of his job.

She didn't know what to do at that point, so like most young adults, she did what came naturally and said the first thing that popped into her head.

"Why don't you ever correct the cafeteria lady when you order in the morning?" she asked.

This left Blake confused. How did she know the cafeteria cooks got his order wrong in the mornings?

"Why do you ask that?" he responded.

"Well, in the mornings you order a random assortment of food, along with a bagel with the butter melted on top, but every day you get the bagel with the butter on the side. Why don't you ever tell them they got your order wrong?"

This came as a shock to Blake. She had noticed him the same way he had noticed her around campus.

"I'm sure that they're doing their best. There's usually a line and I don't want to ruffle any feathers, you know?"

This made her even more curious about him. "That makes sense, but you're an athlete. Shouldn't you be more particular about what you put into your body?"

"Yeah, but not to that extreme," Blake replied. "A lot of people take that approach and they end up spending more time thinking of things besides the game itself. My old man always told me that in lacrosse, the key is to be smart and stay three steps ahead of your competition. How can I stay three steps ahead if I'm worried about something as minor as butter on a bagel?"

Brittany could not believe her ears. Not only did this guy act like Tony, but now he was saying the same thing to her Tony had all those years ago. Maybe it wasn't a coincidence that they'd both admired each other before they even knew one another. She thought to herself it was too good to be true. She had to test her theory.

"How do you feel about Shakespeare?" Brittany asked.

"To be completely honest, I never really cared for Shakespeare. Something about his stories. He just seems to lose me about a quarter of the way through. Every time."

Oddly enough this was a huge relief to Brittany.

"Oh, okay. It's not that important. It was just a random question."

Now that was out of the way, so Brittany was trying to deflect the response and get back on topic. But she couldn't help but be relieved at the fact there was a difference between Blake and Tony. If he'd turned out to be just like Tony, it might have ended up being a problem in the long run because all of the memories she still carried of her long-lost friend. She still remembered all the good times they'd had together from when they were kids and up until her father had decided she was not to see Tony anymore.

She and Blake continued to talk that day about where they'd come from, about their pasts, about their upbringings, about their likes and dislikes, about what made them happy and about their fears. Brittany had finally found someone she could open up to again and Blake had finally found someone who he felt he could trust.

The two of them clicked on a level neither could have possibly imagined was possible from the beginning. Initially, one would expect for there to have been a courting period of awkwardness and getting to know one another, but not for these two.

For Blake, it was far better than he could have hoped for and he was as happy as he had been in a long time.

For Brittany, it wasn't the same. Though they'd clicked and she felt closer to Blake than she'd had to anyone since Tony moved away, something was missing. It was as if she had the amazing feeling she was soaring through the sky yet again, but instead of truly flying, she was only gliding because her wings were still gone.

Chapter 4

Tony, on the other hand, wasn't as meticulous about letting someone into his life. He wasn't afforded the same connections as Brittany had going into college. He did his best not to let anyone know who he was in the hopes no one would trace back a connection between him and his father due to his father's misdeeds. So for the most part, he was just another regular student. He didn't play on any of the schools' athletic teams and he didn't join any of the clubs. He just went to class, the cafeteria, the library and occasionally the student center. For the most part, he was beginning to come out of his shell again and make friends and talk to people again. In large part this was due to the talk he'd had with his father. He often thought about what his dad had said about having someone else to help him through tough times when they arose and having people around him to help him stay strong.

Nothing influenced this decision more than remembering the look on his father's face while the discussion had happened, however. He'd seen the guilt and the shame on his father's face and knew he'd felt the world on his shoulders., as if he'd somehow felt responsible for Tony's misanthropic behavior. Tony knew in his heart that he'd been that way for as long as he could remember, besides when he was with Brittany. The fact remained, however, that he didn't want his parents to worry about him and he didn't want to add any pressure to their plate regardless of his father's sins from the past. The fact was, his dad still did his best to be there for Tony, and that's all that mattered to him.

So, for the most part, he made a genuine effort to speak to people when they were spoke to him and to make a few friends while he was in college. This decision was only expedited by his current friend Jeremy. Jeremy knew Tony was his meal ticket, so he decided to follow Tony to whatever college Tony chose.

Along with his good grades and the fact that he came from a bad situation, he was assured he would be able to get at least most of his college paid for through scholarships. Even though they were in a new place far away from home, Jeremy still had a knack for being a consummate class clown. Rebellion was just in his nature, but even Jeremy wasn't foolish enough to be as blatantly disrespectful as he had been in high school. He quickly learned college professors had absolutely no problem throwing him out of class, giving him incompletes on assignments and letting him flunk out of college. Thus, his mischief came outside of the classroom.

This would end up making him a lot of friends in college. Mainly fraternity guys who liked to watch him put on a show and who would often dare him to do something they wanted to see him do. Jeremy relished the chance to appease his new friends. Never had anyone appreciated his whimsical and rebellious nature, and now that he had an audience, he felt more comfortable than he ever had when he and Tony were in high school. He did everything from stealing a pen off a professor's desk to burying a golf cart on school property. Jeremy was really a rock star with the fraternities, though he would never ultimately join either of them despite all the requests he received. He often wanted to join, but couldn't because Tony wouldn't do it.

The fraternities had no interest in Tony, but that's where Jeremy's allegiances lay, so he wouldn't do it without Tony being right beside him. So since Tony wouldn't do it, neither would he. This fact didn't stop him from partying and having fun with the fraternity guys, however.

This ended up bringing Tony new friends, as well. Oftentimes people around campus would ask him if "he was the guy who was friends with the crazy Jeremy." Being the kind of person Tony was, he never denied the fact, even though it brought mixed reactions from his peers. Some people chastised him for being affiliated with someone such as Jeremy, some people requested a prank they wanted him to relay to Jeremy (though he never did), some just wanted to know for the knowing, and the last type were those who ended up being the friendliest towards Tony. Most of the time, he laughed with them about how completely opposite he and Jeremy were from each other, and most people couldn't believe they were actually friends, but Tony always explained how they went back to his freshman year in high school.

This often quelled a lot of the curiosity that came his way. When it was confirmed, however, that Tony and Jeremy were opposites, some of them would often stick around and try to befriend Tony themselves. Most of the time, they invited him to hang out and branch out the same way Jeremy did.

Tony knew, however, that his main priority was his schoolwork. While he would go to the student center for a few games of ping pong and conversation every now and then, he always found himself drifting off, never able to fully take his mind off his schoolwork.

This was perplexing to people looking from the outside and he was often asked if he ever had any free time or did anything for fun. He gave vague and generic responses to those inquiries, saying things like, "Sure, I go and relax from time-to-time. You guys just don't see it."

Though in reality, Tony knew he had no interest in branching out. He just couldn't tell people why. It had been his nature since as far back as he could remember. The only person who had ever pulled him out of that shell was Brittany, and she was long gone.

He thought about his old flame from time to time, wondering how she was doing, how she looked and what her life must be like. He imagined she was doing much better now that she didn't have to drag him along, but even those thoughts couldn't deter him from his studies for too long. It was just something he accepted as fact and made sure not to dwell on for too long. He knew all he could do now was build for his future, and that thought made him double down even harder into his books. But he still went to the student center to hang out occasionally when he was asked.

On one particular night, there was someone different in the student center. Tony, being who he was, didn't even notice her in the beginning. He just took his usual route on his way to the ping-pong table. But little did he know Jeremy was up to his mischief again.

"Hey, you're crazy Jeremy's good friend, right?" the young woman asked.

"That depends on what he's getting arrested for this time," Tony replied.

The strange girl gave a faint laugh at Tony's joke. "I think you should know, he might really need to *not* go to the frat party this weekend. I hear that the campus is getting wind of who's behind all of the mishaps and cops are going to be there to try and catch him."

"Really? And where did you hear this?" Tony asked.

"My dad is a cop and I overheard him talking to one of his fellow officers on the phone, saying *they're going to get that crazy kid this weekend.* And I know he's not really a bad guy, so I don't want him to get into trouble."

Tony looked at her for a few seconds to see if she was maybe kidding with him. He quickly realized there was no change in her demeanor. It kind of looked as if she was wondering why he was staring at her the way he was. He did appreciate her letting him know Jeremy was in trouble, though.

"Well, I guess I should let him know as soon as I can," Tony said as he pulled out his phone to send Jeremy a text. "Thank you, by the way. I know you could have kept that information to yourself if you wanted to, so I really appreciate you letting me know."

She exhaled as she said, "You're welcome, but I didn't do anything. If anything, you're a great friend for always having his back. I imagine he can be a handful."

"You have no idea," Tony replied as they both laughed. "What's your name? You've put your neck on the line to help us out and I don't even know what to call you."

She looked away kind of bashfully as she said, "Eva. my name is Eva."

"Well, hi Eva, my name is Tony. Nice to meet you."

As Tony hit send to let Jeremy know what he'd just found out, Tony found himself locked in a conversation with Eva. They talked about where she was from and what had brought her to the school. He completely forgot about his game of ping-pong. He learned about her family and the kind of things she liked to do when she wasn't studying. It seemed as if the more he learned, the more he wanted to know and the more questions he asked. It was one of the few times he'd talked to someone on that level in a long time, aside from Jeremy.

As Tony and Eva were getting to know each other, Tony spotted Jeremy outside, signaling him to come outside. Tony knew it had something to do with the message he'd just sent. He also knew how impulsive Jeremy was, so he figured it was best just to go outside to talk to him. He also knew this meant the end of his conversation with Eva for the time being.

"Is that your friend outside knocking on the window?" Eva asked.

"Yes, unfortunately. If I don't go out and see what he wants, he'll just come in here and start a ruckus," Tony replied.

"I understand. It's fine. He's your friend, after all," Eva said.

Tony, however, didn't want to leave it at just a little conversation and then farewell. "I'll tell you what. How about we meet back here the same time in a couple of days? I would actually like to meet tomorrow, but I have tests in two of my classes in a couple of days, so I imagine I'll be locked in my room all day tomorrow."

"That's perfect. We're all here to get our degrees, right?"

"Yeah that's true," Tony said, and they both laughed again.

"Well, again, I'm sorry, but I promise I'll see you again in two days."

So they bid each other farewell and Tony went outside to see what Jeremy wanted.

"What's up man?" Tony asked as they walked back to their dorm room.

As Tony predicted, Jeremy asked about the text, so Tony told him what Eva had heard from her father the night before.

When they were finally in the dorm, Jeremy said, "Really, she told you all that?" He was evidently shocked that someone who didn't know either of them would go out on a limb like that for him.

"Yeah, man. Honest. I didn't even know who she was. She just stopped me before I was about to play ping-pong and told me what she'd heard."

"Wow. I really owe her one. Wait a second--it looked like you guys were talking about something else when I found you. If I'm not mistaken, you two were laughing."

Jeremy knew his friend and he knew Tony had never really taken enough interest in anyone to actually sit down and have a conversation with them past a certain point. "How long were you two talking?" Jeremy asked.

"Come to think of it, I don't really know. I guess I lost track of time." Tony was just as shocked as Jeremy.

"Wooooow! You actually sat down and had a conversation with someone without having to force yourself to?" Jeremy asked in amazement.

"Trust me, I think I'm just as shocked as you are, Jeremy."

"I sincerely doubt that, my friend. I think I'm going to have to meet this girl. So what's she like? What did you guys talk about that got you so off-track?" Jeremy still couldn't believe what was happening.

"She said that she was born and raised here in the city and she always knew this was the university she wanted to go to, ever since she was little and she saw happy people walking around campus and the pep rallies and the parades they had for the teams before big games or if they won the championship.

"She is a science major, which is probably why that was my first time seeing her walking around campus. To my knowledge, she is a pretty reserved person."

"Just like you, you mean," Jeremy couldn't help but interject after that last comment. As far back as Jeremy could remember, Tony had never taken a serious interest in anyone. Of course, even in high school, when people needed help with their school work or when Jeremy would drag him somewhere, he would talk to people. That wasn't the shocking part. The shocking part was the amount of time he'd spent with Eva. Even as Tony continued telling him about the girl he'd just met, Jeremy couldn't believe his ears. Normally, the only time they'd talk about other people was when Jeremy brought up something about his day.

"So yeah, that's Eva. At least that's all I know up until this point. We're supposed to meet up again in a couple of days at the same time, after I take my tests," Tony said with just a hint of excitement.

"You know, if I didn't know any better, I'd say you're falling for this girl harder than zombies after a headshot."

"Dude, come on. I just met the girl. Don't start."

"Oh, wow. And you're getting defensive. Maybe I should have used an avalanche analogy instead. Hahahaha."

They both got a good laugh out of the conversation that night. It was one of the only times Tony let down his defenses enough to where they weren't having a one-sided conversation about Jeremy and his antics. Jeremy didn't know where this thing with Eva would go, but even he could see this girl was already bringing out a different side of Tony that he didn't get to see very often.

Jeremy never bothered him about it, though, because regardless of whether Tony was always warm and receptive or not, the fact of the matter was, Tony was really the only one who he knew would have his back, the only person who didn't just see him as the village idiot he often was. It was an odd friendship, but one Jeremy knew was solid, nonetheless.

The next day, Tony did what he did best. He studied, secluding himself while doing so. He couldn't help but constantly think about Eva during it all. He wondered if it was a fluke. What if she was only talking to him as a friend? What if she was already taken and she'd bring her boyfriend with her the next time they met? What if she didn't really think he was that interesting and she was just being polite? Most of all, above all of these, he wondered if he could even trust someone on that level again.

Even though he had decided to move on and keep working towards his goals, even he could not ignore the elephant in his mind. Since Brittany, he hadn't really trusted anyone enough to want to get out of his own comfort zone (which sadly was his books). Now that he actually wanted to, he was nervous not only in terms of whether she would be receptive to him or not, but whether or not he would be receptive to her, as well. Inside of a person's soul lay all their secrets. Try as Tony might to suppress this one secret, this was one he could not hide from his subconscious.

Just as he started to get even more nervous, he remembered what his father had said about having someone by his side. He thought about what it would be like to have yet another person in his life he could trust. Someone who was similar to what Brittany had been for him.

He decided he was going to put aside his aversions and just wait until the next night to find out for himself, rather than assuming the worst. After acing his tests, of course. It would be a pretty horrible time for him to try to be happy and converse with someone if he knew he was unprepared for a test and got a low score, by his standards, because of it.

The next day came and it was already an event, at least in Jeremy's eyes. "Get up bro!! You have to be on-point for your test so you won't be tripping out when you talk to Eva later!"

Jeremy's antics made their way into the dorm on this morning as he ripped the sheets off Tony while he was sleeping.

"Have you ever just thought about being normal for a day?" Tony groaned. "You know, just saying, 'Good morning, man. I'm about to go to the café. Do you want anything?' You know, something a normal person would say to their friend when they know that the friend in question has three tests he has to be ready for."

Tony tried to curl up and roll over away from Jeremy.

"Hi. I'm Jeremy. Class clown, village idiot, voice of anarchy, demi-god to the imbecile."

"And you're proud of this?" Tony murmured as he once again tried to roll away from Jeremy.

"Hey, don't mock what you don't understand. It's taken a lot of hard work and dedication to be this idiotic on a consistent basis."

Little did Tony know, Jeremy had a trick up his sleeve. As he put the covers back over Tony, he casually said, "You know what? You're right, I apologize. I shouldn't have woken you up the way I did. I'll be leaving now. I hope you wake up before you have to meet Eva today."

As he walked out and closed the door, Tony couldn't help but mumble under his breath, "Well-played sir…well-played."

Needless to say, Tony got out of the bed shortly thereafter and proceeded onto his normal test-taking routine. He recited mnemonics he had made to remember difficult topics, he crammed for a few more hours with Jeremy while they were eating breakfast and he made sure to keep his mind free of all distractions.

As best as he could, at least.

Tony was more and more pleased with his friend. As the days went by, Jeremy started to really take his schoolwork more seriously, so Tony didn't have to spell out the answers to the extent he'd had to do when they were in high school. So, the day went on and he took all his tests and for the most part, felt pretty good about them.

Now he needed to grab a bite of dinner and go see Eva.

As Tony walked into the cafeteria, he noticed one of the sororities that often-recruited Jeremy to help with their juvenile antics. He didn't think anything of it until he saw Jeremy walking out with the crowd.

Tony walked over to him. "Hey, man. What's going on?"

He had a feeling they were celebrating because they were going out to party that night, but he didn't want to believe Jeremy was dumb enough to go to the party after the message he had relayed from Eva.

"We just had a great idea for the party, man. It's going to be epic."

Tony dropped his head in disgust. "Didn't you hear what I said a couple of days ago? The cops are looking for you they know you've been involved in many of the mishaps on campus."

"Yeah, yeah. But see, that's where the great idea comes in. After I told them what Eva told you, they moved the location of the party so we don't have to worry about the cops. They'll go to one location, while we'll go to a completely different location. Smooth, right?" Jeremy was obviously excited about this recent development.

While he was taking his schoolwork more seriously, he still couldn't resist the allure of a little mischief on occasion. He'd been doing it all his life, after all.

"Okay, man. I'll give you the fact that at least you won't be in the same location, but don't you wonder how your name came up in the first place?"

"Yes, WE did, which is why WE decided to move the party. Someone figured there must be a narc on campus, but since most of the students are going home for the weekend and we changed the party location at the last minute, we're all good, man."

"I have a bad feeling about this. I think you should just lay low for at least this weekend, man. If they don't find you in one location, they'll just keep looking. They haven't caught you doing anything yet, and I do mean YET, if you don't stop."

"You worry too much. I'm telling you it's all good. There's no way we'll get caught where we're going."

At this point, Tony was getting frustrated. He always knew about Jeremy's antics, even when he didn't come back to the dorm bragging all night and day about what he'd done. This time was different, though. This time his antics could land him in some serious trouble, depending on what the frat guys asked him to do.

"You know what? You're right. You're a grown man. Do what you want, man, but when you get caught up, don't act surprised and don't come complaining to me." In Jeremy's mind he was 10-feet tall and bulletproof.

"Yes, mom. I promise," he said.

"Okay, well, I'll see you back at the dorm." The two said their goodbyes and parted ways. That had been an uncomfortable situation for Tony.

While he didn't necessarily want to act like a parent, he knew he had to be Jeremy's conscience from time-to-time when he was acting a certain way. Especially now that Jeremy was doing better about handling his schoolwork. The last thing Tony wanted was for him to go back to how he'd been when they were in high school. That thought would not dominate his mind, however. After grabbing a quick bite to eat, it was finally time for him to go to the student center to see Eva again.

Tonight was the night he was hoping would answer all his questions and put all of his anxiety to rest. He couldn't control it while he was heading over to the student center, though. All his thoughts and fears came flooding back to his mind than he'd had before.

What if she has a boyfriend? What if she was just being nice? Am I even ready for this?

When he arrived at the student center, almost as if the universe was trying to send him a sign, Eva wasn't there. Tony immediately started having flashbacks of having to let Brittany go and how his parents had pretty much told him Brittany wouldn't be a part of his life anymore. He remembered the sinking feeling of depending on someone to be in his life and then them suddenly not being there.

A piece of him knew it was too early for him to feel this anxious about meeting someone and wanting to see someone this badly again, especially someone he'd only met once by chance. So then why did he feel as if he'd been let down by pretty much a stranger, he wondered.

As he walked around the student center, it was the one question he could not answer--why someone whom he'd only met once be so prevalent in his mind and why was he so anxious to talk to her again. It wasn't as if she'd given him the secret to immortality or anything. She was just someone he'd talked to by chance because his friend's life goal was to be the fourth Animaniac. Try as Tony might, he couldn't understand it. Not even a little bit.

The questions persisted in his mind, except now it wasn't anxiety. Now, it was just pure curiosity. They were questions he hadn't found himself asking before, and to make matters worse, he couldn't even begin to understand the conundrum he was in.

While he was lying on one of the couches, a face popped into his view. "Sorry I'm late."

Tony jumped up and slightly bumped heads with Eva.

"Ow!" "I'm sorry. I didn't mean to hit your head or anything."

"That's okay. I shouldn't have surprised you. From now on I'll only plan birthday parties for you."

They stood rubbing their foreheads for a while.

"Well, as I was saying, my roommate went on another one of her, 'You can't leave the room until you help me,' kicks. I tried to get away when I knew it was time to meet you here, but let's just say, physical strength isn't on my list of strengths."

Tony felt a huge sense of relief. "Your roommate is really a piece of work, isn't she?"

"Well she's not a bad person or anything. It's just that there are too many problems which are apocalyptic with her. Everything is an issue. She's just not well-adjusted, I guess. But she is a good person, though."

"Yeah, that's a shame. Not just because I'm involved, or anything. It just seems like if you don't pick up, move forward and move on from certain things in life, then you're going to miss out on a lot of scenery, you know?"

Eva couldn't believe what she'd just heard. She knew Tony was a smart guy, but at that point it was almost as if he was speaking directly to her.

The way that she, herself, had moved on from the death of her mother on top of how her roommate treated every tiny problem like a crisis. It was refreshing to hear a guy who actually cared about more than how pretty she was and why she was still single.

So, they stayed in the student center all night long, learning even more about each other as they spoke more about their parents and upbringing. They talked about their likes and dislikes. They talked about their insecurities and what kept them up at night. What they each hoped to accomplish in life. Eva told Tony she wanted to go to college to make her mother proud because that was what she'd always wanted, but Eva what really wanted was the quiet life. To wake up and be beside someone she knew she could trust and someone she couldn't live without and ultimately to raise a family with. Her career would be important to help her get to that life, but in her mind, the career led back to the family and not the other way around.

Tony admired her even more. He listened to her talk and talk about her dreams and what she wanted in the future. The same way Eva felt refreshed by Tony, he reciprocated. He was happy hear someone with a positive outlook who was so selfless, free from desire and wanting nothing more than to be happy with her life and honoring her mother's memory. There wasn't only an admiration there, but also an immense level of respect. Tony knew then that Eva was someone he wanted to be a part of his life. As the night drew on, they both became more and more fascinated with each other.

They started their night in the student center, but when the student center closed, they walked around campus talking as if there was no tomorrow.

By the end of the night, they were on a bench near Eva's dorm in campus.

"What time is it?" Eva asked Tony.

"Hmmm. Let me see…it's 4:30 a.m."

"Oh wow! I know my roommate must be super worried about me right now," Eva said in complete shock. She knew her roommate already had a bad habit of making every little thing into a situation, and tonight would be no different. "You don't think she'd calm down for one night?"

"Unfortunately, no. Truthfully, I probably won't go to sleep until about six a.m. now because she won't let this go. The girl is neurotic. I swear."

"It's okay. I understand. Jeremy was the same way when I told him I'd be hanging out with you tonight."

"Oh, you told your him about me? That's a good sign, right?"

"Yeah, so much so that he wouldn't leave it alone, though I'm pretty sure I did most of the talking, come to think of it. Anyway, I don't want to hold you back from your lecture. Go have fun with your roommate."

"Okay. Well, here's my number. Text me tomorrow. I hope we can do this again sometime."

"Sure thing. Goodnight, Eva, and thanks for a great night."

"Goodnight."

The two parted ways that night without a goodnight kiss, but they were both thinking about it--what it would feel like to be in the embrace of the other. The feeling of being completely comfortable with someone, to be physically and mentally connected with each other. but Tony didn't want to pressure Eva into doing anything too soon. At least that's what he told himself on the outside. Inside, he was still nervous about moving forward and trusting someone on that level again, but he knew that he had to.

When he went back to his dorm that night, before he went to sleep, he told himself the next time he saw Eva, he would let go and go for it. If the connection was still there, that was. As he was drifting off, he noticed something odd. Jeremy was gone. Then he remembered he was out partying with the fraternity that night, so it meant nothing that he wasn't there. Tony went to sleep.

Tony only ended up sleeping for a few hours before Jeremy walked into the dorm. Shame covered his face.

"Why the long face, Goofy?" Tony asked.

"Because I might get expelled, that's why."

"Wait--what? What did you do?"

"I guess I finally ran out of luck." Jeremy was still trying to hide his shame and avoid answering Tony's question, because deep down he knew Tony was the one who'd told him to lie low in the first place. Not to mention the fact that if he did get expelled, Tony would be the most let down by it.

Tony wouldn't take that answer, however.

"Okay, let me rephrase the question. What. Did. You. Do?" "I took the picture of the dean from the administration office and brought it to the party."

"Okay. As despicable as that sounds, it seems like exactly the type of thing you'd do."

"Yea, well this time somehow, the cops still got a tip on where our party would be held and they swarmed the place. It's kind of tough to hide a mural above a fire when you're completely surrounded."

"You're kidding right now, right? This has to be another joke or another prank."

"Dude I'm dead serious. To make matters even worse, one of the frat guys ratted on me as soon as the cops got around to asking him who took the picture. As if they didn't already come there looking for me in the first place."

"Look man. I'm not sure what kind of mess you're in, but come on man. This is your first time getting caught and they got the picture back. At most, they'll put you on probation, right?"

"What if I told you a mustache magically grew on the picture while it was in my possession?"

"DUDE! Why on God's green earth would you do that? What in your brain said that was a good idea? I know you've done some dumb things in the past, but that has to top them all. When you put it back in the morning, did you not think they would do everything in their power to find out who did it?!?!?!"

"Of course I did! But I figured they wouldn't even have a lead, an idea or any evidence how could it be traced back to me?"

"The same way the party got traced back to you, and the same way the cops knew it was you when they got there, or did you already forget that part?"

"Look man I messed up. Okay. I get it. I didn't mean for it to go this way. I swear if I don't get expelled, then this is it, man, I'm done with the pranking. We'll keep going to classes. I'll stop hanging with the fraternities. We'll graduate on time and go on with life. We'll go get jobs, get an apartment and all that stuff, man. Like, seriously. This is it. I'm done."

Tony didn't want to beat a dead horse. He was furious, but he'd never seen Jeremy this serious about anything before. He could see that, for the first time in his life, Jeremy was showing true remorse for something that he'd done. That didn't stop Tony from realizing something like this would very likely get his friend expelled. The two sat in the dorm talking all morning and planning for what was to come on Monday.

When Monday came, neither of them felt any more at ease about the situation. Taking a picture of the dean and drawing a mustache on it was serious. The dean wasn't a horrible person, and many of the students liked him, but he did have to answer to the police on this one, so he would have to make an example out of Jeremy. Both Tony and Jeremy waited on pins and needles for his scheduled meeting with the dean. They recited the speech and speaking points they'd prepared that they thought would give Jeremy the best chance of remaining in school.

Chief among those was Jeremy's grades. He had maintained better than a 3.0 and had a great attendance record since he'd enrolled, and he would revolve his plea for lenience around those facts. After some last-minute role playing, the time came for Jeremy to go see the dean. The two agreed to meet back at the dorm later that evening, Tony wished his friend luck and they both went on with the day. Tony went to his classes while Jeremy was in his meeting. Tony couldn't help but be concerned for his friend. While he knew deep down in his heart that Jeremy probably would receive a harsh punishment for what he'd done, he didn't want his friend to have to go back home for good because of it. He kept thinking about all the progress Jeremy had made since he'd first met him and knew something like this could derail all of it.

It was really bad timing for a situation like this to come about. All he could do was hope and pray for the best, but for the time being, he couldn't bring himself to focus on anything else. He didn't even answer his messages from Eva. As optimistic as he was trying to be for the sake of his friend, he couldn't help but expect the worst.

When the time came for Jeremy's meeting to be over Tony was waiting for him on the steps.

When Jeremy came out, Tony could tell by his face that the punishment that he was to receive wasn't good.

"What did he say?" Tony asked anxiously, but for the first time since Tony had known him, Jeremy appeared to be speechless.

The two waited a few seconds in silence before Jeremy finally said, "He said I was expelled for two semesters. He was tempted to ban me from the campus for life, but since I've been a good student in the classroom, he granted me leniency outside of the classroom."

"What are you down for, man? That's great news! This could have been a whole lot worse. Trust me, man. A year will fly by in no time and you can come back."

This news excited Tony. All day he'd been expecting the worst, that being a lifetime ban from the school. Somehow, his best friend only got a two-semester suspension.

Under the circumstances, Tony could not be more excited.

Jeremy, on the other hand, was not as excited as his friend. While he knew he would likely be suspended, it didn't set in until he heard the words spoken aloud. While Tony saw the year passing by in a flash, all Jeremy could think about was the year without the only true friend he'd ever known--the only person who didn't see him as the obnoxious, overbearing, annoying class clown. He felt like he'd let Tony down.

Then there was the year apart he had to consider. Their hometown was too far away for him to come visit the campus regularly. Not to mention, it wasn't as if he was rolling in money to begin with. The option of making constant trips was non-existent.

Then it hit him…while he was gone for a year, Tony would advance a year. So by the time he returned, Tony would be a year ahead of him. That would mean a year in college without Tony. Jeremy had been taking his classes more seriously, but he didn't know how to function scholastically without Tony's help.

"Hey man, are you okay?" Tony could see Jeremy had spaced out. "Yeah. I'm just thinking about how much it's going to suck to be back home for a year."

As nervous as Jeremy was about his situation, something about Tony's optimism made him calm down a bit. Maybe Tony was right. Maybe this year would fly by quickly. Then he could return to college and get back on track and finish, and only have to spend one semester apart from Tony--if he worked hard enough. He figured even if Tony wasn't there for his last semester, he could still pull it off.

"So, when do you have to be off campus?"

“By the end of the week. But I’m going to leave ASAP, before something else happens while I’m on campus.”

“Well, I’d like you to stay as long as possible, but I understand. That’s probably for the best. You have a lot of heat on you now and you shouldn’t take a chance that you’ll get burned again.”

The two shared another awkward silence before Tony finally said, “Come on. Let’s go back to the dorm. I’ll help you pack. Like I said, man. Two semesters will be gone before either of us knows it. Then you’ll be back, and we can both finish up.”

Then it hit Tony the same way that it hit Jeremy. That would be two semesters without his best friend, and even then, after those two semesters, he would graduate earlier than Jeremy and have to wait another year before his friend would catch up.

However, Tony didn’t know that Jeremy had already come to this realization. He also knew he and Jeremy came from an inner-city school and he knew what kind of life awaited Jeremy if he didn’t finish college and make a better life for himself.

He decided to keep that information to himself and keep speaking optimistically toward Jeremy, keep encouraging him to do the right thing.

“So are you still done? Done with all of the pranking and all of the jokes?”

"Huh, what gave you that idea? I said that if I *didn't* get expelled then I was done."

"DUUUUDE!"

"I'm just kidding, Tony. Yes, I'm done. I just want to get this next year over with so I can come back here and finish what we started."

Neither of them knew how the next year would go. Since their freshman year in high school, rarely a day went by when they didn't influence each other's decisions.

Tony influenced Jeremy more so than the other way around. Tony had a single mindset since he was a child, and not even the losses his family had suffered nor the downgrade in the school system had deterred him from this path.

And he was still on it, as far as he was concerned.

Jeremy, however, had been on a dark path before he'd met Tony. It was mostly Tony's constant pushing and guidance which, over time, had brought Jeremy around to seeing there might be a better life for him than he'd initially thought he was capable of achieving. Even now, the optimism he had for his situation was in no small part because of Tony. While neither was aware the other was thinking it, they both knew this next year would be a trial for Jeremy.

Chapter 5

For Brittany, the next couple of years were eventful in their own right. As Brittany grew closer to Blake and they both were getting closer to graduating, life was good. They were known as the *first couple* on campus and even won homecoming king and queen at their college. While neither of them particularly cared for the added attention, they decided not to be rude about it, either. They'd decided they weren't going to stop seeing each other or hide the fact that they were an item so the best thing for them in the long run was to just embrace it. After all, it was a college campus. It wasn't like high school, where they would be getting looked at in the hallways.

They just had to deal with the occasional teasing and bantering about how perfect they were together. There came a day near the beginning of the fall semester where they seemed to be getting a little more attention than usual, which seemed odd to both of them. After all, by that time they'd been dating for years.

Most of the attention eventually died down, but they didn't let that ruin their day. They continued on like it was business as usual. They went to their classes, Brittany hung out with her friends, Blake went to practice and they ate together. On their way to the student center, they were walking and talking about life after college, just as they had done on many occasions--though this topic became more frequent the closer they came to graduation.

"Do you really think your father wants to turn the company over to you one day?" Blake asked. At this point, they were thinking about where they would go and where they would live after college.

"Well he's never come out and said it himself, but my mother always told me he eventually wants to."

"Has she ever mentioned when he might retire?"

"Not really. She says he loves his job and he's very proud of how far along the company has come under his watch. I think if anything, he might want to pass the torch and teach me everything he knows to make sure the company stays in the family."

"You know, I actually wouldn't mind living in your home city. My mom has a branch of her business there, as well. I'm sure I could get a job there, too. Plus, there's so much to do, and with there being so many people there, we would be able to live our lives and hide in plain sight. If that's something you would want, that is."

"Well of course it is. If anything, I'm worried about you and how you will fit in."

"Oh, don't worry about me. It will be great. We can go to the top of one of the skyscrapers and go to a professional football game. Hey--I hear your city is pretty well-known for its Shakespeare-in-the-Park performances in the summertime, too. Right?"

Brittany instantly had a flashback to her last summer with Tony. She thought about all the times they'd had as children all the way up to that point and started to wonder how Tony was doing, where he was and if he was okay. She thought about what such a shut in he was and how he'd always had his nose in a book. She thought about how he would come over and help her with her classes sometimes, even when he had homework of his own. She thought about how selfless and kind he always was to her and her family. Then she thought about the night in the park, the first time they'd kissed. She thought about the ring he'd gave her. A ring she still wore on a necklace around her neck to this day.

She had told Blake about it, but only that it had come from an old friend. She'd always avoided going into detail about it. She couldn't help but wrap her hand around it as she thought about the past.

"Hey…hey…Brittany…are you still with me?"

"What?!?! Yeah, sorry. I just spaced out a little."

"Yeah, I can tell." Blake was a little thrown off by it. He had never seen her space out that hard before, but he figured maybe he was just seeing things.

"Ummm…I guess you could say we're known for Shakespeare-in-the-Park. A lot of tourists come to the performances while they're in town." Brittany finally got herself back on topic.

They both came to a stop by a fountain near the middle of the school. Brittany looked into one of the buildings and turned around to find Blake down on one knee, holding a ring in his hand.

"Brittany, will you marry me?" Blake asked anxiously.

Brittany was shocked by the proposal. Not so much that he'd proposed, but it was just so sudden and she just wasn't prepared. She didn't know what to do. She didn't know what to say. She was just stuck.

As she opened her mouth to say *yes*, another flashback of the night with Tony came flooding back to her mind…

A part of her still missed Tony…she knew a part of her would probably always miss Tony.

She also knew Blake made her the happiest she'd been since her father had banished Tony from her life.

"YES!!! YES I WILL MARRY YOU!!!"

As Blake jumped up and hugged her, two photographers, along with all of the friends they had made since they'd started college, all came out of hiding to congratulate the two of them on their engagement.

Brittany was taken off guard. She'd thought they were alone on their walk. Needless to say, she quickly discovered that wasn't the case.

"How long have you been planning this?" Brittany asked, still in Blake's arms.

"Well, you remember a couple of months ago when we went to play a game about 30 miles from where you grew up? I tracked down your parents and talked to them about it. I asked them if I could ask you to marry me, and they approved. After that, it was just a matter of waiting for the right time to ask you."

Brittany still couldn't believe everything that was going on. The fact that so many people had taken time out of their busy days to watch Blake propose to her was more than a little flattering. As the two sealed their engagement with a kiss, the photographers snapped their photos to give to the newly-engaged couple and to submit to the school paper.

Blake didn't particularly care for their milestone being plastered all over the school paper and yearbooks, but it was the only way he could get great pictures which hadn't been taken by a random camera phone.

After the kiss and the photo, the two shared hugs and handshakes with their friends. As far as they were all concerned, it was only a matter of time before Blake and Brittany got engaged. That didn't take away from the celebration they were all having. After a few hours, they all went their separate ways and left the two to talk to each other again. But there was no doubt this particular event would be the talk of the campus, at least for a couple of days. As the two found themselves alone again, they talked about telling their parents and sending them photos of what had just happened.

They talked about wedding plans, as well. Thankfully, like most other things, they agreed on what they wanted. They didn't want to be the couple who waited a long time for their wedding. Since both parties and both of their parents agreed their children were making a good choice, they decided to have the wedding before they graduated. Since they graduated late that April, they decided to have the wedding in early April, which was only a few months away. But since neither of them was really the *grand wedding* type, they had plenty of time to get all the arrangements together before their wedding.

They knew the hardest part would probably be getting all of their friends and family there at such an odd time during the year.

"While we're on the subject of our parents, what exactly did my parents say when you asked them if you could marry me?" Brittany couldn't be happier with how the day was going and the wonderful surprise Blake had for her, but she couldn't help but wonder exactly what her father had to say about her getting married. "We just talked for a little while about my future plans. Your mother was happy. She said that we made a great couple and she was glad we found each other."

"And my father? What did he have to say about it?"

"He congratulated me on my decision and told me about how he felt before he asked your mother to marry him. He said he respected that I came and got their approval beforehand."

"That couldn't be all he had to say."

"Well, after that we just talked about my future plans. You know, where we're going to live, where I plan to work, internships, credit and all that good stuff."

"Ah, okay. That sounds more like him. I'm glad he approved, though. He really must like you."

"Why do you say that?"

"I know firsthand he can be very…calculating. If that's all he grilled you about, then you really must be as special as I've always thought you were."

"Brittany, I know you've told me you and your father don't really get along very well, but you've never told me why. I don't mean to push, but he seemed like an ordinary father to me, maybe even better than most. Why do you two not get along?"

Brittany wasn't sure what to say. A piece of her got stirred up towards Blake, thinking he was taking her father's side, but she knew Blake was just wondering for curiosity's sake. He wouldn't try to crawl under her skin for no reason. Heck, they barely even argued beyond the minor scuffles about politics, business practices, etc. That knowledge, however, did not help this particular situation.

Even if that were the case, she still had to come up with an answer for why she'd always resented her father for exiling Tony out of her life. She'd never told Blake about Tony and had made it a personal point even to avoid subjects involving him--which left her in her current predicament. How could she tell her fiancé she despised her father for telling her she could no longer see a guy she'd loved nearly a decade ago?

She couldn't. Because even though it was real to her, it wasn't fair to her fiancé. She didn't want him to have to deal with her baggage or feel he was competing with someone she'd never see again.

"We're just two different people, I guess.

"Mom and I have always been peas in a pod. Dad and I just couldn't seem to click after a while."

"Well, I guess I can see that. You kind of remind me of your mother a little bit. She was really cool about the whole thing, and at the same time she was as happy as she could be."

Brittany still wasn't completely okay with her father being included in their decision to be married, but Blake was a good and genuine guy and he wouldn't do something like running off with her without asking her parents first. It just wasn't who he was.

That was all in the past, though. For now, she would choose to focus on what a great day it had been for both her and Blake. Blake's parents were excited about the pending nuptials, as well. They knew about their son's shy nature, though they didn't know why. They often wondered whether he would be able to handle the responsibilities of running the family business or not due to his passive nature. They were passive aggressive in nature, which didn't help Blake's confidence.

They were always finding different ways of telling him he had a responsibility beyond himself, but they never asked him directly if he wanted to be a part of the business, nor did they try to get to the root of his shyness and try to help him overcome it. No--both his father and mother were all about business all the time.

Brittany often marveled over what a miracle it was that he'd turned out as humble and well-adjusted that he did. News that their son had come out of his shell enough for him to find a woman to marry not only made them happy for their son, but it made them optimistic about him accepting his role of keeping the family business in the family and running the company when the two of them were ready to step down.

Now all that was left was to get both of the families together for the big day, which wasn't as big of a deal for Brittany as it was for Blake. Brittany's parents had always been there for their daughter's big moments and Brittany's father had no problem delegating his daily duties to his board in order to be there for Brittany and her mother.

Blake's parents were different. With them always needing to have a hand in everything going on in the business, they often found themselves putting their business before pleasure. Oftentimes that pleasure extended to their son's school events.

Knowing this, Blake made a day, set it in stone and was sure to let his parents know in advance that they were only going to get one chance to watch their one-and-only child get married, forcing them to make the ultimate decision between business and pleasure.

Brittany offered to work around their schedules, but Blake loved Brittany and he wasn't going to let anything stand in the way of that, not even his own parents. He wanted this day to be about him and Brittany, but mostly Brittany. She was the most special person in his life and he wanted to make sure this day would be about her and no one else. He decided to take a gamble with an ultimatum to see if that would get their attention. Little did he know the gamble would actually pay off.

After Blake told his parents there was absolutely no way he would move the wedding date, his parents made him a solemn vow that they would clear their schedules and be there for his wedding. Blake was more than excited about this news, but he knew better than to expect anything until he saw them both there that day.

In the coming days, Blake and Brittany both anticipated the wedding with great anxiousness. It was hard for them to focus on their schoolwork. Even without the abundance of the social responsibilities that most people had--friends, gathering of the families, parties, etc., they found themselves short on time when it came to maintaining their schoolwork and planning a wedding.

Their only saving grace was that they wanted it to be small and private, so they didn't really have to be on the phone with decorators all day.

A couple of months passed, and the day was upon them, the day when they were finally to be wed. They were both as nervous as they could be. Most of Blake's anxiousness was him anticipating something he never even thought about before he met Brittany. He still couldn't quite believe he'd found her. Between his absence of friends and the lack of attention he'd received from his parents the thought of having someone always by his side was both intimidating and wonderful.

Brittany's trepidation, on the other hand, wasn't as noble. The truth was, since the day Blake had proposed, she thought about Tony from time-to-time. She wanted to marry Blake…she loved Blake…Blake made her happy. So why couldn't she stop the memories from flooding back into her mind about a boy she'd known nearly a decade ago? It was something she had been struggling with since that first day. Unfortunately, due to the summer's events and the disdain she developed for her father because of it, she had become very good at hiding her emotions.

Blake never suspected a thing, through no fault of his own. He was a guy who never really had an abundance of human interaction outside of high-school sports and his college lacrosse matches, so he couldn't be expected to be able to see past Brittany's façade. Nevertheless, Brittany still could not quite get Tony's memory out of her mind. She knew she would never be with him.

For years now, she had been at ease with the fact that she would never see him again. There was nothing in her that believed otherwise. She never wanted to completely forget the great times she'd had with him. After all, he had known her longer than anyone and they'd grown up together. Forgetting him would be no easier than forgetting her entire childhood, which was why she kept the ring he'd gave her around her neck. She never wanted to forget about the friendship, but right now, the feeling was not one of missing an old friend.

As she sat in her dressing room looking at herself in her wedding dress with her bridesmaids, her mother walked through the door, almost as if she could sense her child was struggling with something, which wasn't uncommon for her. Her mother was her best friend.

"MOM!!! I'M SO GLAD YOU MADE IT," Brittany exclaimed as she went over to hug her mother.

"Of course I made it, dear. You know I wouldn't miss this day for the world."

With everything going on that day, and with everything going through Brittany's mind, she couldn't help but shed a tear.

Assuming that they were tears of joy, Brittany's mother said, "Oh, now why are you crying? I'm the one who should be crying. My one-and-only daughter is getting married today. You look so beautiful in your dress, dear."

Then Brittany's mom started to cry as they both looked at each other and hugged one another. Even the bridesmaids started to cry at the sight.

"Hey ladies, can you give my daughter and me a minute alone, please?"

"Sure thing," they all said as they left the room. After waiting for them to gather their things and depart, Brittany's mother couldn't help but ask, "What's wrong, dear?"

"Huh? What do you mean?"

"Brittany, I'm your mother. Always have been, always will be. I know when there's something on my child's heart."

Even after all those years and all that practice, there was still one person on the planet from whom Brittany couldn't hide her true emotions.

Her mother was very intuitive in that respect. She had poured her life into Brittany since the day she was born. It was no mistake that they weren't just mother and daughter, but best friends, as well.

"Well, truthfully, it's nothing. It's not really important. Just something I've been thinking about lately. But like I said, it's nothing."

"How about you tell me what it is, and I'll decide for myself if it's nothing or not, sweetheart."

"Okay, but promise you won't tell Blake. I don't want him feeling bad about this--or anything."

"I promise."

Brittany still didn't know if she should tell anyone else about what had been on her mind, but she had vented to her mother her entire life, so why stop now?"

"You remember Tony, don't you?"

"Yes, dear, how could I forget? He was always such a good boy, and you two were such good friends."

"Well, the day Blake proposed to me, before he actually got down on one knee, we were talking about where we would live after we graduated, and my hometown was one of the places mentioned. He was talking about all the attractions it had to offer, and one of the things he brought up was

Shakespeare in the Park. Then I started thinking about Tony again."

"I see. That was the night he gave you that ring and kissed you, wasn't it?"

"Yes, it is."

"So why is his memory frightening you so?"

"I don't know, Mom. It's not like I think I'll see him again, or that I don't love Blake, but for some reason I haven't been able to get that night off my mind since Blake proposed. I've been trying to figure it out and nothing makes sense.

"Again, I don't think he'll burst through the doors and I'll run off with him or something silly like that. It's just that, I don't know, I feel as if there might be something I'm missing--something I'm supposed to see and I just can't see it, you know?"

Brittany looked at her mother, who was smiling. This immediately sent Brittany into a state of confusion.

"What happened? Did I say something wrong?"

Her mom was her usual calm self.

"Sit down, dear. I've never told you this, but your father is having an affair."

"WAIT, WHAT?"

"I'm just kidding. Your father wouldn't do that."

"Why would you do that to me right now, Mom? I about had a heart attack."

Brittany couldn't help but laugh at her mother. Even at a time like this, she hadn't changed a bit.

"I thought that you could use the laugh. You want to know what I think?"

As Brittany nodded, she couldn't help but fear what her mother might say. What she might think about Brittany still holding onto her keepsake and her memories after all this time.

"I think you still need to learn to forgive. It's fine for you to hold onto your memories, dear. Your father and I met Tony and his parents when you two were only babies. Even though you haven't seen him for so long doesn't change the fact that you've still known him for most of your life. Forgetting him wouldn't be any easier than forgetting me or your father--or your entire childhood, for that matter. You two were practically joined at the hip most days. It's perfectly fine that you want to hold onto his memory, but you're still focusing on the pain.

"The reason these memories still scare you is because you're still thinking about the *what ifs* and *what could have been* instead of focusing on all the good memories you two had together and just letting that be what they are. Memories. Now, I could very well be wrong, but I'd be willing to bet it wasn't just the *Shakespeare in the Park* that brought the flashbacks. You're not taking into account the fact that a second guy was giving you a ring to show he loved you, are you?"

At that moment, Brittany couldn't help but wonder if her mother was right. She really hadn't thought about the issue of the ring. She'd been so focused on that night at the park she never realized that Blake giving her a ring might have been making her wonder if that's what Tony would have done someday if her father hadn't banished Tony from her life.

"That's what I thought. It's time for you to forgive, dear. Forgive your father, forgive Tony's father, forgive fate and move on. I can't tell you how glad I am that you still hold onto those memories you have from your childhood. It lets me know my baby is still alive inside of you. Yet and still, that doesn't ignore the fact you still haven't yet learned to forgive.

"What happened between you, Tony, and your father was horrible, and I wish I could have done more to prevent it, but it's done. You can't go back and undo what happened in the past, but what you can do is push forward and be happy with what you have been blessed with in the future. Besides, Tony was always a very smart kid. Even you must admit there's a good chance that wherever he is and whatever he's doing, he's doing just fine. Knowing him, he still thinks about you, too."

After everything her mother just said, everything her mother was able to glean from just one small moment in her life, Brittany couldn't help but start crying and hugging her mother again.

So many times she had been there for Brittany when she thought the world was over and she needed answers. Not one time did she ever turn her daughter away or shirk away from telling her something for her own good. Brittany couldn't help but be thankful for what a wonderful mother she had.

As the day went on it, was finally time for the wedding to start.

Blake might not have gotten the quality time with his parents that Brittany had, but he was just as happy, nonetheless. His parents showed up. He saw them walking in to take their seats as he was standing at the altar waiting for his bride. To him, that was, soon to be the second-best gift of his life. Minutes later, the flower girls paved the way for Brittany as she walked down the aisle.

When she got to him, he was already shedding tears of joy. The sight of him made her cry, as well. The occasion was a happy one, and the few people who attended were all at a loss for words at the two of them at the altar saying their vows. They had each written their own vows and everyone agreed they were heartfelt and solemn vows.

This was love. The wedding couldn't have been more perfect for the two of them. The reception after the wedding was also a success. They got to talk to family and friends, and everyone congratulated them on a very bright future they were sure would accompany the two of them.

Blake's mother shared her embarrassing tales, and Brittany's father issued his threats--jokingly of course. It was a very happy occasion, and everyone got their jokes in. As the night began to wind down, friends had to go their separate ways on account of the fact that finals week was soon approaching. The families also had to go their separate ways, due to many of them being business owners or managers. Blake hugged his mother and shook his father's hand and bid them safe travels on their flight back home.

Brittany hugged her father and thanked him for coming. As she went to hug her mother, they both pulled each other in tight as her mother said, "Don't forget what I told you, dear. I'm so proud of the woman you have become. Remember what I told you, and know I will always love you, no matter what."

"I love you too, Mom. Don't worry. I will do my best to remember everything you've told me. I love you sooo much."

The two of them finally let each other go as Brittany bid her parents safe passage on their trip back home, as well.

The newlywed couple stayed behind. They spoke about how great the wedding was. More than that, they couldn't believe Blake's parents held true to their word. They both joked about how

Blake had probably cashed in his one lifetime favor with them.

At the end of the night, they departed back to the hotel they had booked. They could have gotten into married housing, but with them leaving the campus soon, they didn't think it was worth the bother of moving--not to mention because they were still in college, there would be no honeymoon.

At least not immediately. For the night, the hotel room would be their getaway, but they didn't need the luxuries of a cruise or a beach to enjoy their first night as a married couple.

They ended up staying the night at the hotel. A couple hours before dawn, Brittany got a call on her phone. She didn't want to answer any calls from anyone while she was with Blake on their first night as a married couple, but she noticed the number was one she didn't recognize, and it had the area code of the city that she was from. So she answered.

At this point Blake had rolled over and was staring at his wife.

"Are they okay?!?!" Brittany asked with a shaking voice.

Blake was very concerned for his wife at this point.

"What's wrong?" he asked.

Brittany suddenly hung up the phone. She scrambled around in a panic, grabbing her things and getting dressed.

"What's wrong? What is going on, Brittany?" Blake still wasn't sure why she had been spurred into such a sudden frenzy.

"We have to leave--right now."

"What, why?"

"We have to go. We have to go to them."

Blake jumped out of bed and grabbed hold of his wife. "What is going on???"

Then he noticed that Brittany was crying. He grew even more worried than before. "You can tell me anything. What's going on?"

"My parents…We have to go to them. Please. We have to leave…" she sobbed.

"Why? What happened to your parents?"

"They said that my parents were involved in a car crash…a drunk driver ran a red light and T-boned them…"

"Oh my God! Are they okay? Did they make it to the hospital?"

"They made it back to the hospital. My father is in critical condition…but the crash was on my mother's side. Oh, God. She didn't make it…"

Blake didn't know what to do. As he held her, he knew he had to get her up and they had to leave immediately. He got her things together and guided her out to the car. They drove for hours and hours to get to the hospital where they were keeping her father, but little did Blake know time was not on his side. Brittany was slipping further and further away.

She couldn’t stop the tears from flowing at the loss of her mother and her best friend. During the whole drive, she didn’t reminisce on the wonderful memories she had made with her mother through the years. She just kept wondering why this had to happen to her mother. Her mother was a great person with a heart of gold. Moments like these were when she needed her mother the most, and now, without her, Brittany felt all alone. Even with Blake there by her side she didn’t know how to put the weight on him the same way she would have with her mother.

Blake just kept driving as fast as he could to get her there. He talked a little bit during the drive, trying to console her. He let her know he was there for her, but she just ignored him for the most part. After a long morning of driving, when they finally made it to the hospital, they were escorted to Brittany’s father. He was just getting out of surgery. He wasn’t conscious yet, but they sat by his bedside, waiting for his eyes to open while the nurse told them about what had happened to Brittany’s mother.

It was as they had told Brittany on the phone. The car was hit on her mother’s side by a drunk driver who had sped through a stop sign and hit the car. According to the report, her mother was dead on impact. The nurse said the blame was completely on the drunk driver.

Brittany couldn’t help but look at her father. Resentment built in her heart. She thought about the two people who meant the most in her life at a given time had been taken from her on her father's watch. Tony, after they'd kissed at *Shakespeare in the Park* and became a couple for the summer. Then her mother, after she had been there for her at her wedding when she'd needed her the most.

She knew in her mind her father would never get into a car crash on purpose, and he certainly wouldn't put her mother's life in jeopardy if he could avoid it. They'd loved each other, and nothing had ever come between them for all the time Brittany was around them.

Her heart was another story. In her heart she just kept feeling as if somehow her father could have avoided this. He could have stayed in a hotel for the night, he could have hired a driver and he could have stopped and just let the car speed by.

Even though everything about the incident said that the drunk driver was at fault she couldn't help but think there was some way her father could have avoided this. When her father woke up, the first thing he asked was, "How is my wife?"

No one wanted to be the bearer of bad news, but everyone knew it had to be done. The nurse stepped forward and explained what happened. After she told him, he started to cry uncontrollably. He, like Brittany, felt as if it was all his fault. He ran through the same sequences as Brittany about what he could have done differently. For days he could not eat. He had visitors but he never said much.

Brittany stayed by his side for an entire week after her mother had passed, and her father found different ways to apologize to Brittany for what he'd done. Brittany tried to quell his guilt, telling him it wasn't his fault--it was the drunk drivers' fault. But the news she had passed on was nothing short of catastrophic in his eyes. Eventually, Brittany had to go back to college. It was within her means to miss finals week due to her mother's passing, but she wanted to finish and get through school.

She told everyone that's what her mother would want her to do, though, in reality, she didn't want to be in the room with her father anymore. His constant apologizing, coupled with Brittany's already present thoughts of the part he'd played in her mother's death became too much to bear.

She felt if she stayed by his side too long she'd start hating him. So she left. Her father had his share of visitors in the hospital. Some old friends and college buddies. Some of them were his business partners. They all wanted what was best for him and told him he should take a break for as long as he needed until he could get his head on straight and go through his own grieving process.

As the next week went by, he spent his days thinking about the advice he'd gotten from his friends and colleagues. He spent his nights thinking about his departed wife.

As for Brittany, thankfully, she was well prepared for her classes.

She did a lot of studying before her wedding, anticipating that afterwards her time would be spent doing other things. She never imagined what would actually happen, though. After she passed all of her tests, the day came when she was to walk the stage. All of her friends were there for her and she got a standing ovation as she walked the stage. Blake couldn't have been prouder of the woman he'd chosen to be his wife.

Her father couldn't be there for it, which she completely understood. Although he did find a way to leave her a graduation present. One of her friends walked up to her with an envelope, claiming a man in a suit gave it to her, and told her to pass it to Brittany.

When she opened it she found a key inside, along with a letter.

My dear, I'm sorry that I couldn't make it to your graduation today, but make no mistake--I'm so very proud of you and I know your mother would be, as well. We both watched you grow up to become a fine young woman, and your mother and I both were given the gift of watching you become what I'm sure will be a fine young wife. I'm sorry for everything which has gone on recently.

I've spent many nights contemplating what could have been different these past few weeks. I know you hate hearing me apologize for everything that happened that night, so I won't say any more about it. You are a strong woman. You're smart and you're driven. It's because of these things that I know that you will be great. The key I have given you is to my office at main branch of the company. As of midnight tonight, you will be the sole owner of the company. I will be going away for a couple of months to try to get my life right. I trust your studies and your experiences have taught you much in these past few years. I'm also confident my colleagues at the company will make this a smooth transition for you if you choose to stay with the company and not sell. I love you very much, my dear. More than you will ever imagine. I'm so proud of you, and good luck.

"BLAKE!! Look at what my dad just sent me."

While Brittany's life was taking off in drastic fashion after graduation, Tony's was dealing with a loss of his own. Nothing compared to what Brittany was going through, but he was slowly losing his best friend.

As the next year went by after Jeremy's departure from campus, Tony spent all of his free time with Eva. Without Jeremy, there she was the only person who he really had a connection with on campus. Eva didn't mind it one bit. They would talk in the student center and walk around campus talking about life. They even became fans of the school's sports teams, which was totally out of character for Tony.

Tony texted Jeremy frequently that year, doing his best to keep in touch with his best friend. They texted each other during the day. Tony wanted to know how it felt being a working man back home, and Jeremy wanted to stay in touch with the one person who he considered a real friend, too.

But as Jeremy's yearlong suspension drew to a close, Tony got fewer and fewer texts from Jeremy. It was strange to him, but he tried not to think much about it. He just waited patiently for his friend to tell him he was on his way back to the campus that summer. That summer was no different from the school year for Tony.

He spent most of his time with Eva, and since it was Eva's hometown, he even met her father, which went over better than Eva had thought it would. Eva's father was really receptive of Tony. When they weren't around her father, Eva would joke that he was either glad to see Eva liked someone enough to bring him home or that his cop senses didn't sense *punk kid* when Tony walked through the door.

Either way, they were both happy for his acceptance. That would be the only highlight of Tony's summer.

He waited and waited for that special text from his friend and it never came. The first day of the following semester, he got a text from Jeremy.

Hey bro. I didn't enroll in school this semester. I might come back next semester, but I got a good job and I want to see where it goes.

Tony texted him back immediately, trying to get him to reconsider his decision, but his texts were met with no reply.

Tony wondered what was going on with Jeremy, but without their messaging he had no way of actually finding out. Even Eva was confused by Jeremy's absence. Tony didn't want to lay his problems on her, though. He just told her that Jeremy missed registration and changed the subject. Eva, being the intelligent girl she was, knew there was more to the story, but she also knew how reclusive Tony could be when he was upset. For now, she chose to leave it alone and go with the flow of Tony's conversation.

Time passed and Tony stayed steadfast in his studies, as he always had.

Jeremy never came back to college the following semesters. After he missed the second time, Tony knew not to expect Jeremy to re-enroll. He knew better than anyone how erratic Jeremy could be. So rather than ask a series of questions which would force his friend to continue lying to him, he decided to just let the matter be.

Tony went on to graduate summa cum laude and valedictorian of his class, and because of that fact, he was quickly headhunted by a large marketing company. The strange part was that it was in his hometown.

After talking it over with Eva, the two decided it was a good move. He would enter a big company at a higher position than most and she could get a teaching job at one of the local schools.

Tony wasn't certain he wanted to accept the offer. He knew he deserved the job, and he knew he would excel, but that was all secondary when weighed against the fact that he would be working in the same business community his father once had. Tony didn't want to be looked down on by his peers, and he certainly didn't want to feel like people were always talking about him when he walked by.

He couldn't worry about that, however. This was the best job offer he received. He knew in the long run, doing well at a job like this would put him head and heels over someone else his age, so he accepted the job. With the decision being made, he and Eva packed their things, said goodbye to her father and headed back to Tony's hometown.

Chapter 6

After all his years of focus, Tony's hard work was finally paying off. His job was everything he'd thought it would be plus some. It was extremely tedious and required much of his time in the beginning, but he didn't mind. For him, it was pretty much doing what he'd done since he could remember. Except now he was getting paid for it. He went work and studied his assignment then came home and studied it even more to help his firm get the most out of their proposals.

He didn't necessarily want to be away from Eva as often as he was, but she didn't mind it as much as he did. She knew he was just trying to do his best, as he has always done. She made Tony agree that on his days off there would be absolutely no work. So long as he kept to that rule, she remained the encouraging girlfriend she always had been to him over the last couple of years.

Being in Tony's hometown was an adventure for them both. Eva finally got to meet Tony's parents, and they were all delighted to meet each other. When Tony told them the news about the new job he had accepted, they couldn't help but be proud of everything he'd accomplished. They knew more than anyone how hard he'd worked to get the opportunity that had been presented to him.

They all had a family dinner to celebrate, not only Tony's return and his new job, but also to celebrate Eva being in his life. Tony's father didn't know if his son would take heed to what he'd said before Tony left for college, and now to see him with someone who was close enough to him to move away with him was nothing short of amazing in his eyes. He knew more than anyone how much a hardworking man could benefit from having a great woman by his side, and that's what he wanted for his child, as well.

Now that Tony had that great woman, his dad was relieved. There was another concern on his mind, however. He, like Tony did when he was considering the job, knew Tony would be caught in his shadow in some way, eventually. Though Tony was his own man and an adult now, his father couldn't help but to try to protect his son. After dinner, he asked Tony to go take a walk with him while his wife and Eva got to know each other a little better. Even though Tony kind of feared the bedwetting and crybaby stories his mother might tell Eva, he agreed to his father's proposal.

When they were outside, Tony's father stared at his son with pride. "I'm very proud of you, son. You know that, right?"

"I know, Dad. I couldn't have made it this far without you and Mom. You two have always been great parents."

"You don't know how happy I am to hear that from you. After everything I put you and your mother through, I felt like I failed the both of you."

"It's okay, Dad. You didn't fail. You made a mistake. Everyone does."

"Well, that's actually what I wanted to talk to you about. The world you are going into, it was my world. I know how those people can get. They are money-hungry, greedy, and all they speak about are profits and margins."

"I kind of had a feeling it was like that, but it's okay. I'll be sure to watch my back. I learned a lot while I was in college and I think I'll be okay."

"College can't train you for what you're about to deal with, son. How you deal with what comes next will be a testament to what you've learned outside of the classroom. Unfortunately, there are no books about how to deal with deceit, betrayal and espionage."

"It can't be that bad. There are good people in the business world. They aren't all sharks, right?"

"Son, I think it's time I tell you exactly how I lost my job and everything I'd worked for back then…"

"No, Dad, it's okay. I didn't need to know back then, and I don't need to know now. All I know is you have been a great father to me and a great man to my mom. I never believed you did all of the things they said you did."

"Okay. I'll trust you. You've always stayed out of trouble in your own way. I will say you're right about people in the business world. They aren't all sharks. You will meet some good people and make some great connections while you're working. It's not them you have to worry about. It's this consumer-based world that we live in, where everyone wants what they want when they want when they want it.

The people who you have to worry about are those willing to step over anyone to get what they want. Gluttony has become the newest heavenly virtue, and the sharks who are in your waters are never full."

For the first time, As Tony listened to his father's words, he thought about asking his father what he'd done that had gotten him into trouble all those years ago. A man as wise and as kindhearted as him? It didn't seem as if he would do something illegal.

Tony thought about his father's words and took them to heart. Maybe his father was one of the sharks he was referring to and he'd lost his way somewhere. Maybe he'd regained his mind and his heart after he was caught--which could explain why he was warning Tony about other people he might encounter in the business world. Whatever the case might be, he decided his father had shown plenty of contrition for what he had done. No need to make him re-live it all again. He decided to cling to what he always had. His father loved him and always treated him and his mother as well as any man could.

"Do you understand, son?"

Tony had drifted off into his own thoughts for a while.

"Yes. I understand, Dad. You don't want me to fall victim to the world, right? Don't worry. A long time ago you told me to find someone, and I did. I wouldn't betray her for the world."

"I'm glad to hear that. Words can't express how proud of you I am. Most kids would have shut down when put in the position I put you and your mother into. You just kept pushing and kept fighting. Your mother and I always talk about how special you are. Don't ever let anyone tell you that you're not."

As Tony's father brought his gaze from the sky, he saw his son smirking he grew vexed. "What are you smiling about?"

"Well, there are a lot of men who lost their jobs and killed themselves, killed their wives, became hermits, abandoned their families and just ultimately shut down when they were faced with what you had to face. Yet here you are, still being a good man to my mother and a good father to me. You say I'm special for staying the course. I say I was just taught well."

Tony's father ordinarily harbored a perpetual feeling of shame, but after hearing his son's words, all of it washed away. He became filled with pride and relief. Relief that through everything he'd put his son through, he'd still become a smart, kind and hardworking man. He couldn't help but hug his son tighter than he'd ever hugged him, doing his best to fight back the tears so he didn't cry in front of his only child.

The two stayed out for a little while longer before they headed home. While Tony and his father were out having their talk, Eva and Tony's mother were engaged in their own conversation.

"You know, I've never known my son to feel so comfortable inviting people to meet us. You must be a very special woman. How did you two meet?"

"His friend was planning on doing something stupid, and everyone on campus knew who those two were. Jeremy because of his antics, and Tony because they were always seen together. Tony was probably the only real friend Jeremy had, but I was trying to pass on a message that there was trouble heading Jeremy's way. Tony and I talked for a while, and after that, everything else just fell into place."

"That's interesting. As calculating as my son can be, it's odd to think he would just let something fall into place on its own."

"I know. The more I got to know him, the more I kind of wonder about that myself."

"If anything, my son is patient and persistent. If I had to guess, after meeting you myself, I think he just knew a good thing when he saw it."

Eva thanked her for her comment. She felt an overwhelming relief that Tony's parents were so receptive of her.

Tony didn't really speak of them too often while they were in college. Not in a way that would suggest that they were bad parents. He just stayed to himself and he never went home for the spring and summer breaks. The only times she could remember him leaving campus were when he went home for Christmas, which only happened twice. When he'd come back, he would just tell generic stories that he'd gone home, saw his parents, ate food, had his smiles and came back. For most people, that would be farfetched, but with Tony being the hermit he was, it was totally plausible. Which was why she didn't feel the need to pry. But that didn't take away from her wondering whether they would accept her or not.

"So, tell me. How was my son while he was in college? He came home a couple of times, but he never really spoke of it much."

"Believe it or not, that's probably because he didn't have much to talk about. Tony is a very hard worker. He was always studying to make the best grades he could, or looking into a topic he thought was interesting. If he told you his college life was uneventful, it's because it was.

Come to think of it the only time his life ever veered off course is when Jeremy was getting into trouble."

"Yes, I think Tony brought him by once or twice. He was always a playful young man, but according to Tony, he was a good boy, and I decided that's all we needed to know."

The two women went on to talk about other experiences they'd each had in college. Talking about the needy roommates, the smell of five different perfumes wafting through the air in the mornings, never knowing whose side to take in roommate battles…it was very strange to Tony's mother that life in a women's college dorm hadn't really changed all that much.

"I worry about him, you know. My son."

"Why is that?"

"He's more like his father than he realizes."

"What do you mean?"

"He has a heart of gold. He puts the world on his own shoulders, and he gets so focused at times that he doesn't see the danger around him. It's what makes him a great man, but it also led to one of the darkest moments in his father's life. I worry that Tony's obsessive nature will cloud his vision like it did with his father."

"What do you mean? What happened with his father?"

"If Tony hasn't seen fit to tell you himself, I don't feel it's my place to divulge that information."

"That's okay. I understand. You don't have to tell me."

"Well, I may feel that it's not my place, but in the best interests of my son, I feel I have to. Especially since you're the closest to him."

So, Tony's mother went on to tell the story of what had happened to her husband at his last company.

Eva couldn't believe it. The man she'd met earlier that night didn't seem like the type to get caught up in something like that. She listened on the edge of her seat for the entirety of the story. The more Tony's mother spoke and the deeper she got into the story, the more she realized what she meant when she said that she was worried about Tony sharing the same fate as his father.

They weren't absolutely the same in every aspect, but what made Tony's father successful happened to be a collection of the same dominant traits she saw in Tony every day.

"So that's what happened to his father." Eva was still stunned by the whole thing "I can't believe it. He's such a kind and wise man. It doesn't seem as if anything like that would even be an issue for him, and yet, I see where you're coming from. I may not know your husband that way, but Tony is almost the same way most of the time."

"Yes, and that's what worries me. I am glad that he found you, though. You're obviously an intelligent woman, and you care for my son very much. There is no greater joy that a mother can have for her son than to see him with someone who will love him every day. However, I must ask you to keep that story between us."

"Yes ma'am I will. But may I ask why?"

"Tony has never asked about his father's descent, so I can only wager he doesn't want to know. And if he doesn't want to know, it's not our place to force the tale on him. What I will ask is, since you're now aware of the fate which could befall him, that you'll do your best not to let him come to the same fate his father did. Keep an eye on him for us.

"He works hard, just like his father, and we don't want to take that away from him due to sheer paranoia. I guess what I'm saying is save him from himself, but only if it's necessary."

"Yes ma'am. I have to say, Tony is very lucky to have parents like you two."

As the two women were wrapping up their conversation, Tony and his father made their way through the door. They all stayed in the living room and talked for a little while longer.

Eventually, Tony and Eva decided it was best if they left and went to their apartment. It was getting late, and Tony had to get ready to work for his new company. Eva had to get ready to teach her class, as well. She had gotten an offer to teach at one of the schools in the same district as Tony's former high school. So they bid their farewells and headed off into the real world to start their careers.

Back at Tony's parents' house, his mom and dad couldn't help but feel great for Tony and Eva--

but that's not to say they didn't share the same concern about Tony's fate.

"What did you say to Tony while you two were out?"

"I just warned him about the world he was going into and we talked for a little while. Our son has become a wise man while we were away."

"I always knew he would be. I told Eva about what happened with you at your old company."

"Good. That's probably for the best. Tony isn't interested in what happened, but he doesn't realize he's going down the same road. It's probably good for his sake that he has someone close to him who can steer him clear of that fate if the road opens itself to him."

"My thoughts exactly. I didn't want to tell her before Tony brought it up himself, but given the circumstances, I thought it was necessary."

"OH--I FORGOT!! I have to tell my beautiful wife I love her. Have you seen her?"

Tony's mother hit him and smiled. Through it all, she'd always known her husband loved her more than anything. That was one fact that wasn't going to change on that day or ever.

Over the next couple of years, Tony and Eva continued to grow together. Eva's students adored her. She showed her students love and compassion. She was also known to show tough love whenever necessary. She was a truly great teacher in her own right. She elected to go into the math department. In the two years she was at that school, she had already garnered the respect of her peers for her commitment to her students and their success. She might not have had the corporate prestige Tony did, but she worked just as hard, and sometimes even longer hours than he did, if she had multiple tutoring sessions. By all accounts, she was truly changing the lives of her students and putting them on a better path. Tony couldn't have been prouder of his girlfriend.

She not only had the verbal support of her students, who had voted her *Teacher of the Year* both years she was at the school, but her students also had the best test scores on the state exams to show the difference she was making scholastically. Tony was her biggest fan, always reminding her how he wished he'd had a teacher like her when he was in school.

While Tony might not have been changing lives on the scale that Eva was, he was making a difference at his company. His superiors quickly realized how sharp and dedicated he was and brought him in on a couple of key projects in his second year with the company. His peers were very impressed with his ability to quickly grasp the concepts of the projects and his dedication to every detail of the brand marketing strategy.

More days than not, when he was invited in on the project, he would come in the next day with ideas on how to make the strategies more effective.

While not every idea was implemented, his bosses never tried to temper his enthusiasm.

Tony had quickly worked his way up to a junior marketing consultant. It was no secret he was going to be an inside marketing consultant within the next couple of months, which was a big deal. He would be the youngest in the office by far. Ordinarily, this would breed resentment among peers, but in this case, no one questioned the move.

When everyone went out for lunch, Tony would be working. When everyone went out for a beer and to watch the game, Tony would be working. It was no secret he had tremendous work ethic. He even helped his co-workers with their jobs when he could. He was the nice kid of the office, and he wasn't upset by that at all. It would remain that way for the coming months as he continued to put on display all his hard work from college and his hard work at the office. He learned all that he could so he would be ready for any opportunity should it arise.

While Tony and Eva were focusing on their respective crafts, Brittany was making her presence known as her father's successor at their family's company. Throughout the business world, her father was known as a generous man. He focused on the relationships he formed with the people he was negotiating treaties with, more so than he focused on grabbing every dollar he could. For this, he was heavily favored by his contemporaries. This mentality made it so his company continued to grow due to the information he gathered and the favors he cashed in on at moments when he felt it necessary.

Brittany, on the other hand, had a different approach. She knew most of the companies her father dealt with depended on them to continue their own success. She used that leverage to get what she wanted from companies she knew depended on them. As one would expect, this fostered a lot of resentment. The companies expected her to be like her father had been and when she wasn't, they would often remind her that her company had come to prominence because of her father and his business practices. However, Brittany didn't see them as allies the way her father had. She saw them as sources of revenue.

She quickly became known for her strong-arm tactics. Tactics which when met with mention of her father, were even further exacerbated. No one knew the hidden resentment Brittany had for her father, and because of Brittany's insistence over the opposite conclusion, she wasn't even aware of the malice in her heart. As much as the board members wanted their old friend back, or at least to temper Brittany's rampage through their business world, they never said a word. As much as they despised Brittany's behavior, the fact was, she was bringing in a lot of revenue for their company.

They all believed her conduct towards their colleagues was deplorable, but as long as she kept increasing gross profits and stock shares at the rate she was, they accepted her behavior. With Brittany being the head of a multinational company and her father leaving her to her own devices, with her mother resting in her grave and the board at her company endorsing her every decision, there was no one policing her. Blake, her husband, fought tooth and nail with her regularly about her change in behavior since taking over the company.

Brittany pushed back just as hard as Blake did. She always told him she was doing what she must for the sake of her family's company.

Blake knew it was more than that. The woman he'd married was slipping away, and he was doing everything he could to hold onto her. He was doing his best to pull her back to the surface. Unfortunately, every attempt he'd made had failed. As much as he wanted his wife back, he had not yet been able to reach her. This didn't stop him from trying, though. While he couldn't be completely sure, he figured somehow that Brittany's change had a lot to do with the death of her mother, which was even more apparent when she refused to reach out to her father to check on him and see how he was doing.

The truth was, Blake didn't want to believe the woman he married was even capable of alienating the man who'd raised her. However, he couldn't ignore the facts. She'd clearly grown more distant since the death of her mother—and not just from her father, but from everyone. Her employees couldn't talk to her. Her distant relatives and best friends couldn't get through to her, either.

Worst of all, he, her own husband, couldn't get through to her. As reluctant as he was to admit it, the only way he could get his wife back was to convince her to forgive her father and move on from the death of her mother. He couldn't see a way he could go about doing so, however.

Brittany was a completely unfamiliar person now. In all their years of dating in college, he'd never known her to be as stubborn as she was being. When he reached out to her friends, he quickly discovered she'd either met them in college or they didn't know her very well in high school, claiming she had always been kind of shy and distant in high school. Not in a bad way, just very reserved. Blake couldn't believe that. The Brittany he'd known in college was always very friendly and welcoming. She might not have actively gone out seeking new friends, but she was never opposed to talking to someone new if they initiated a conversation with her.

This made him wonder if something like this had happened to her in high school, as well. Unfortunately, there was no way to figure out her problem without asking Brittany directly. One day, when she came home and she was in a particularly foul mood, they started arguing again.

"What is the matter with you?" Blake said.

"Wow, are we on this again? Let it go, Blake," Brittany snapped in a dismissing voice. "Yes, we are going to be on this again, and again, and again, because you go to work every day and you come home pissed off almost every evening."

"It's a stressful job, okay? The board doesn't want to get behind me on a business proposal I'm trying to get passed with one of our competitors," Brittany explained. She tried her best to keep everything related to work but she knew Blake meant there was something deeper than work going on with her. But that didn't mean that Brittany wanted to talk about it. She continued to deflect.

"Look, Brittany, you know that's not what I meant. I've seen you stressed out plenty of times in college, but you never let it get to you."

"There's a difference between cramming for an exam and running a company."

"It's not about the company. It's about you. It's almost as if you're looking for new ways to get upset."

"Blake, I already have to deal with a room full of men who get on my case at work all day. Now that I'm home, you're doing the same thing."

"Well, since we're all about pointing out differences today, there's a difference between having concern for your wife and trying to protect your stock shares."

"What do you want from me?"

"I want to know what happened to my wife. I want to know why your friends from your own wedding have never before seen you this way, but you're trying to convince me this is just how you handle things." Blake didn't want to bring up that her friends were worried about her, but it was all he had left to try to convince her she really had an issue.

"What do you mean *my friends*?"

"Your friends are worried about you too, Brittany. None of them can get in touch with you and in the rare instances they do, even they notice a change in your speech."

"How? I talk to them the same way I always have. Maybe I'm not able to talk as long because I'm busy, but it's not like I'm shutting them out or anything."

"Brittany did anything bad happen to you in high school?"

"What are you talking about now?"

"None of your friends from high school really know this side of you, either. They say you were very reclusive and barely socialized with anyone when you didn't have to, but you never had a mean streak, even then."

"So you've been talking about me to my friends?"

"That's not the point and you know it."

"Oh, please. Do us both a favor and get to the point."

"Did anything bad ever happen to you before the death of your mother? Something in high school that made you shut people out, kind of like you're doing now?"

Brittany only paused a moment, but to her it seemed like forever. Up until that point, when she was working was the only time she had forgotten about her father's past transgressions. She had forgotten about her old friend. She knew what Blake was getting at and she had no rebuttal for what he was insinuating.

However, that hadn't lasted long before she thought about her mother, her mother's memory and the last thing her mother told her about forgiving her father and moving on. She thought about her mother and what her mother would have wanted, but she knew she couldn't forgive her father. It had been over two years since her mother had passed and she still couldn't quite shake the feeling that her father was the main antagonist in her life. Which was why any mention of the man put Brittany in a state of anger. Whether it was with the people she was doing business with or her husband, mentioning Brittany's father usually didn't bode well for anyone.

Blake couldn't let it go either, though. He wanted the Brittany back that he'd met in the cafeteria in college. He wanted the wife back that he'd married. He was well aware his probing was building resentment within Brittany, but every time he thought about letting it go, he decided to try again just one more time, believing this would be the time he'd break through.

Unfortunately, Brittany still wasn't ready to harken to her mother's words.

"What does that have to do with anything, Blake?" Brittany snapped back.

"Everything… nothing…I was hoping we could talk about it and you could tell me," Blake pleaded.

"There's nothing to tell. If they told you I was reserved in high school, it's because I was. Since my first day of high school, that was the case. Nothing BAD happened to me in high school to bring that about." Which was, actually, the truth, and Brittany knew that was the case.

Which is why she used that particular play on words--to try to avoid the conversation.

But Blake was persistent. He just kept pressing.

"What about before that? Was there anything?"

"You know what? I'm done with this conversation. I told you I'm fine. If you don't want to believe me then that's your choice."

As Brittany began to walk away, Blake wanted more than anything to yell at her and make her sit down and talk about whatever it was she was hiding.

He couldn't. He didn't know why, but he couldn't.

That was the moment he knew that he was no longer going to try to poke and pry to figure out what was wrong with her. Her mother was the only one who could ever get through to her in this state, and she was gone.

So now all Blake felt like he could do was support her and wait for her to realize it on her own. He didn't know how long that would take, but at the moment, he truly felt that was his only option.

So that's what he would do. Just sit back and wait.

The coming days didn't make anyone any more optimistic about Brittany's attitude changing for the better. She still attacked her meetings and negotiations with fury, sometimes even more than she previously had, and just like before, no one challenged her on anything she did. She was surrounded by people who enabled her every step of the way.

Her advisors tried to warn her she was making more and more enemies every day. She didn't care. Even when someone said something that went against Brittany, she'd shoot it down immediately, leaving absolutely no room for defiance. So, as was the case before their attempts at helping her restore her sanity, as long as she was bringing in profits to the business, they let her do what she wanted and stood behind her in her decisions, even when they didn't agree with her behind closed doors.

Tony ended up encountering his antagonist, as well. One day out of the blue, he ran into Jeremy. Tony hadn't heard from Jeremy in years, since before his graduation. He had a little bit of a feeling something was going on with Jeremy, but Jeremy had been his best friend for years, so he decided to believe Jeremy bore him no ill will. After all, it might be good to catch up with an old friend.

"Tony! What in the world is up, bro? How have you been? How's Eva? Did you guys end up graduating? Wait. Why are you even in this city? I know you graduated. Heck, you're you. Are you in trouble?"

Jeremy sent a barrage of questions at Tony and Tony found it flattering and reassuring, because that was definitely something his best friend would have done.

"Whoa, hold on! Slow down! Ha-ha. Everything went well. In fact, it's going better than I planned. I'm now working with a great company. It's hard work, but I figure after a couple of years at this job, I can move on to bigger and better things, you know. How have you been though, man? I've been back in this city for a couple of years now and I haven't seen you around."

"Yeah, I left for a little while. Been on a career path myself," Jeremy said with the utmost pride. "I was asked to go run a store in another city and turn it around. I'm proud to say we got it done.

"So, yeah, like you said, in a couple of years, if I can stay after it, hopefully other good things will happen for me."

Tony was shocked. He'd thought for sure that Jeremy would return to his old city and fall back into old habits, but apparently, he'd been doing pretty good for himself.

Tony couldn't be any happier. "Man, that's fantastic! I never thought I'd see the day you'd be happy working for the man."

"Well, you know, we all have to grow up one day. Plus, if this keeps me from going back to that dump of a neighborhood I lived in when I was in school, I'd say it's worth it. Right?"

"Absolutely," Tony agreed. He couldn't believe the words coming out of this new Jeremy's mouth. It's almost like getting kicked out of school had been a good thing for him. He'd certainly grown up in their years apart. One thing was for sure--he was not dealing with the same Jeremy.

"Hey. I have some time on my hands. How about we go grab some lunch?"

Chapter 7

Tony's success soon faced a test like one he'd never seen before. There was something shady going on at his office and he couldn't quite put his finger on it. He'd noticed a few of the higher ups were showing him a little more favor than the others in his group. At first, he chalked it up to his hard work and thought maybe another promotion was in the works. He wasn't entirely unfamiliar with such a thing his short tenure with the company.

But this time was different. Something just wasn't right. Then he thought maybe it was paranoia. With all the chatter in the office about how fast he was climbing the ladder, it was possible he was just seeing shadows.

"Hey, man," said Johnny, one of Tony's office mates, startling Tony in the process. "What are you doing spacing out in the middle of work? That's not like you."

"Huh? What do you mean? I was just thinking about what I should be doing next," Tony said, trying to deflect suspicion.

"Whatever, man. Well you might want to pull yourself together. One of the bigwigs will be here in an hour or so. If I were you, I'd put on my focus hat," Johnny said.

"Wait, why are they coming here?" Tony asked nervously.

"We don't know. I'm going to go out on a limb and say you didn't check your company email. That's where the rest of us saw it. It just says they will be here in an hour, so we are all to be on our best behavior while they're here," Johnny said with a little concern in his voice.

He could tell something had gotten into Tony's head. He just couldn't figure out what.

"Okay, thanks for letting me know, Johnny." Tony said.

Now Tony started wondering what kind of questions they would ask him and what he should say to those questions. He wondered if they would even talk to him at all or if he was just concerning himself over nothing.

Either way, he figured there was no harm in preparing himself for an interaction with the higher-ups in the company. For all he knew, it could lead to another promotion in the near future if he impressed them enough. So, for now, he chose to heed the side of caution.

That proved to be the right decision, in his mind. Once they made it to the building everyone went through the proper introductions. From what he could tell, he wasn't treated differently than anyone else. It turns out they'd come to talk shop with Tony and the others. Bill, the CFO, and the highest title holder in the group, came to ask about how the firm had been so successful as of late.

He also wanted to know how they planned on continuing that success. At first it was a broad conversation to everyone present, but the deeper the conversation went, the more Tony stood out to him. As Tony had expected during his preparation for the visit, it wouldn't hurt to look over the company's numbers and look at how they were trending. When the Q&A was done and the visit was essentially over, everyone gave their proper goodbyes and went back to work as usual.

Tony followed suit. As he sat down at his desk, however, one of the men who was with Bill came up to him and said, "The CFO has requested that you meet him in the lobby. Follow me."

Tony was taken aback. He didn't know what he had done. He thought he had answered all of Bill's questions in an acceptable manner. As he was coming around the corner to the lobby, Bill awaited him with a smile.

"Hello, your name is Tony, isn't it?"

Tony was even surprised that someone like Bill remembered his name.

"Yes sir." Tony said, slightly confused.
"Don't look so confused, son. You impressed me up there and I wanted to talk to you face-to-face. If that's okay with you?" Bill said with a reassuring smile.

"Oh, yes sir, that's fine. I just didn't understand why you chose me out of all of the people in the room," Tony said.

"It's because you stood out. Almost every question I had, you had an answer for--and not just any answer, but a mindful answer. I could tell you did your homework. That's impressive, especially for a kid your age," Bill said.

"I do my best, sir," Tony said.

"I'll tell you what. How about I put your mind at ease? I'll tell you the truth. My reasons for coming here were twofold," Bill explained with a smug smile on his face.

"Okay, sir. What really brought you here?" Tony asked, trying to appear reserved.

"Firstly, I really did come here to ask you all a few questions to see what has made you all so successful recently. What this office is doing here is not going unnoticed at the corporate level. We want to figure out what you are doing right so we can incorporate those ideas into the practices of the company as a whole," Bill said.

He looked at Tony, waiting for him to respond.

"Okay, that makes sense. What was the second reason?" Tony asked, still keeping himself reserved. "Secondly, I wanted to find someone to help us on a larger business proposal we are handling. I need the smartest guy in this office to come and sit in on a project with us. You know, work some of the magic for us one time. Of course, you will be compensated for your time and efforts if you agree," Bill said.

Tony was shocked and didn't really know what to say, but he knew this could lead to another promotion and better help his future if he could impress the right people.

"If you believe that's me, sir, then I'd be more than happy to help."

Tony's response made Bill very happy--enough to invite Tony out to diner to further discuss Tony's role in the deal. Tony was excited for the opportunity. From the moment he'd said yes, he had already started thinking about schemes and strategies without even knowing into what market they were going. All he knew was this was his big break. This was his opportunity to be a rising star in the company and set him and Eva up for life.

When he got home that night, he couldn't wait to tell Eva the big news. She was sitting on the couch reading when Tony came in.

"Eva, you will not believe what happened to me today."

Tony didn't even have the time to slow down for small talk, he was so excited.

"Well, what happened? Tell me!" Eva said as she put her book down to give Tony her full attention.

"The CFO of the company came by our office today because our team has been doing so well. He came by to ask all of us what we have been doing to close out so many second-looks and deals over the past year."

"Really? So how did it go?"

"Oh, it was great. He asked all of us in the room for our opinions, but afterward he called me out of the room to speak with me privately. He said I made an impression."

"I believe that. You've made it a point to learn that job in-and-out when you first got there. I'm sure you know a lot more now than you did back then."

"Yeah, but here's the crazy part. He invited me out for dinner and it was great. We talked about an upcoming bid they're putting in on a project for a new client and he wanted to find someone new to bring to the team to familiarize themselves with that account and eventually take charge of it. He believes this will be a HUGE win for the company!"

"That's great, Tony! Well, what made him choose you out of everyone in that office?"

"When he came by and asked all of us the questions about our recent successes and got feedback from everyone, apparently my answers really stood out to him. Then when we went to dinner, we continued our conversation and he decided I was the right man for the job."

At this point Eva couldn't have been prouder of Tony. She, more than anyone, knew how hard Tony had worked to advance and set him and Eva up for the future. Maybe even a future family. They hadn't gotten around to talking about when or how many kids they wanted. All they had agreed on at that point was they both wanted kids.

Yet and still, she couldn't help but hear Tony's mother's voice and the story she'd heard about Tony's father and wondered if Tony was on the same road of destruction.

For now, however, she decided this might very well be a wonderful opportunity and she was just being overly cautious.

"It's about time that someone other than me noticed," she teased with a smile. Tony went on about Bill for another couple of hours, saying how the CFO had told him about all of the things he'd be able to do if he did a good job at the higher levels of the company. The only thing which appealed to Tony was that he was on the road to one day running the company and changing his family's name.

Brittany, on the other hand, was finding herself as stressed as ever at work. Blake had become distant since their last argument a couple of months ago, and she knew it was due to the last argument they'd had. In her mind, she was happy he'd stopped drilling her about every decision she made.

At the same time, though, she felt uneasy in her stomach about it. She'd flirted with the idea that maybe she felt bad about leaving things the way they were. Maybe Blake was right. Maybe she was being an angry little girl and lashing out. She'd thought about these things more often than she would care to admit.

The problem was, as soon as she started thinking about her past decisions, she would get to a point where she thought about her father, and that made her uneasy.

She didn't know where her dad was or how he was doing. She knew she could easily hire someone to find out. She occasionally picked up the phone to try to use some connections to hire a private investigator, but ultimately, she'd put down the phone as quickly as she picked it up, convincing herself she was busy and she could do it later when she'd finished what was in front of her.

The problem with that idea was there was always something in front of her. Today was no exception. For the last eight months or so, she'd gone into business with one of the largest machine producers in North America. She knew having him in her back pocket would facilitate a lot of acquisitions in the future. When companies built new structures, they went through her partner, and if that company wasn't willing to do business with her company, she knew she could jack up the prices on the machines they needed for their new construction. Her partner, however, had conditions of his own for the partnership.

"Are you actually always working?" Jesse asked as he entered her office.

"Do you ever knock?"

"Your secretary said you were busy, but I told her it was urgent."

She sighed. “I suppose that’s fine. I was just wrapping up here, anyway. What can I do for you?”

“I just thought I’d come tell you *Will & Will* caved. They’re ready to talk about making you one of their sponsors. They say you’ll have to do it for the same rates as everyone else, but hey, the wheels are in motion.”

“Good. It’s about time. They just should have sat down with us in the first place. If that’s all they were worried about then this was a waste of time. I’m willing to pay the price.”

Brittany had gone through similar disagreements with other clients in the past, but only a select few. She never quite understood it.

“Not everyone in the public eye has a positive view of you at the moment.”

“Well, that’s their problem. I’m not a criminal and I haven’t broken any laws, so they’ll just have to get over whatever they think they know about me.”

“Are you insinuating only criminals do bad in this world?”

“No. But, I will suggest you choose your next words wisely.”

“Oh, come on now. Don’t be so testy. Seeing as how we’ve had so much fun together in our…partnership. Speaking of which, once again, I held up my end of the bargain. So how are you going to hold up your end this time…my place or yours?”

"As much as I'd love to have a heart attack wondering if my husband would walk in on us, I actually have a yoga class I have to get to. Which is why I was finishing up as you walked through the door."

"Oh, don't try to split now. A deal is a deal," Jesse said as he stroked Brittany's hair.

Brittany softly grabbed his hand and said, "Oh, trust me, I'm not running. I'll make it up to you. I can't have my favorite machine tycoon getting any ideas about forming a new…*partnership*, can I?" Brittany said as she turned and walked away.

As she was getting into her car, she let her driver know the destination and texted her husband Blake.

On the way to yoga, be home soon.

As she arrived at her destination, she got out of the car and handed her driver $50, bidding him adieu.

She then walked to her destination.

"Well what took you so long?" a man asked, opening the door to her knock.

"A business meeting ran a little long. A client didn't agree with a particular piece of our arrangement."

"Oh, really? Don't tell me you're already losing your touch."

"Baby, the only thing I want to touch right now is you."

Then the door closed behind them.

Ever since they'd returned to the big city, Brittany had not been herself. Inheriting her Father's company so suddenly, coupled with her mother's sudden passing, was too much to absorb. Then, without her best friend, as well, she was truly lost.

She wasn't just having one affair, but two. Jesse was just a means to an end. This new guy, however, was for pure pleasure. An excuse to get away from the people who truly cared about her, the people trying to pull her back from the abyss. Brittany's heart was in sorrow. No one could ever understand the kind of turmoil she was going through internally. As for now, she would remain lost. Physically she was present, but it was almost as if her soul no longer had an anchor on which to attach itself. It was for the taking for whomever gave her the comfort she craved at that given moment.

When she went home to Blake that night, she got a surprise she never saw coming. That day, Blake's bosses had wanted him to go out and show a client around town, to help him imagine the possibility of doing business here and everything the city had to offer.

What he did not expect was to see his wife's car. When he initially drove by, he'd thought nothing of it. Then it struck him--his wife's yoga class was in the other direction. At first, he thought the driver was just driving around while he was waiting on her, but something in him couldn't shake the curiosity of why he'd seen her car so far away from her yoga studio.

What was the driver be doing so far away from her studio when, the fact of the matter was, Brittany could decide to leave the studio at any time? Which meant if she wanted to leave right now, she would have to wait at least a half an hour for him to get back. Anyone who knew Brittany at all knew she would rain down fire for such tardiness. Although for all he knew, she was in the car.

That evening, Tony went out with Eva to celebrate her birthday at her favorite restaurant. She wanted to do something which gave the two of them time together. Since they had officially become adults, they weren't able to see each other as much as they'd had in the past. Eva had requested that they have a night together to spend time and talk like they'd used to.

Which was probably for the best. In the past, Tony had to surprise Eva a couple of times, but the surprises had gone awry in one way or another. Eva was always happy nonetheless, but it bothered Tony. She saw how hard he tried and the effort that he put into being a good boyfriend and she'd grin from ear-to-ear--not to mention the fact that she usually got a couple of embarrassing stories about Tony out of his attempts.

Now they were at her favorite restaurant. Tony pulled out the chair for her as she sat down.

"This is so great. I love this place! They have such good food and they always have the best paintings on the walls. Do you remember one we were looking at the last time we were here?"

"Yeah, I think so. The one with the animals, right?"

"Yes sir, it had the white bird with the black snake in its claws while the snake wrapped around its body in the air. There was a black elephant stomping on one lion and getting bitten by another on the coast, and then a white octopus with its tentacles wrapped around a black shark that was biting it."

Eva and Tony had looked at that picture for most of their meal, discussing what it was supposed to mean.

Eva, still drawn to that particular painting, asked, "Did we ever figure out what it meant?"

"I don't think so. There was so much detail in that picture I think we just left and agreed to disagree."

"That was such a great painting. I remember you were saying it was supposed to signify balance, like yin and yang."

Which was how Tony's analytical mind saw the painting.

"And, you said it was supposed to be about how we may all be different and in different stages in life, but everyone has their own fight."

Which was how Eva saw the painting.

Eva was a deep thinker. Rarely did her thoughts on a matter ever stop on the surface. There was always something more Eva found interesting when there was a lesson to be learned.

"I mean, think about it. The eagles eat snakes, yet the snake is wrapped around the eagle. And sharks prey on octopi, but this one is strangling the shark to death while its being bitten. It's as if they're all trying to win their fight and survive. And they're all opposites," Eva said, trying to plead her case to Tony.

"Hello. My name is Travis I'll be your server today. Do you guys want to start off with drinks and an appetizer, or do you already know what you'd like?"

Since they'd been to this restaurant before, they already knew what they'd order.

They proceeded to tell Travis what they wanted.

After the fact, Eva asked Travis a question. "By the way, Travis, do you remember the painting you guys had of all of the black and white animals on that wall a long time ago? What was the painting supposed to mean?"

Travis let out a small laugh. "Well, if I told you it would spoil the fun. I'll be back with your food shortly."

As the waiter left, Tony and Eva fell back into their discussion.

"You know, that painting makes me wonder about…how do we know what's supposed to be right and what's supposed to be wrong, you know?" This brought Tony into her world.

See, Tony was capable of seeing more. He was just never very fond of it. Since Brittany had been taken from him, he'd never known how to put into words what he'd wanted to tell his parents. He'd tried over and over again to tell them how he felt. How he'd wanted them to talk to Brittany's parents. How he'd wanted to ride the train across town to visit. How it wasn't fair that a mistake not his own could cost him so much.

Then he woke up one day and realized something he would never forget. He'd realized that life went on. In the middle of trying to work up the courage to ask his parents why, he'd gotten school supplies, started school and even made a new friend. He'd made a new goal--getting a high-ranking position to convince Brittany's dad he deserved to be with his daughter.

Time passed, however, and while Tony's upward trajectory continued, his hope for reuniting with Brittany had been lost. He'd continued to go to school, age and even make another new friend. Regardless of what was going on in his life and how much he wanted things to change, life went on.

"I think we all know what *right* is on most things. We've known what *right* is for thousands of years. The rest, like the picture, is decided by our perception. Like how a bad person can get killed and some rejoice, while others pray for their soul. There are many things that are inherently wrong and yet we find ourselves flirting with both sides on a regular basis, never fully deciding just to do right for the leeway to do wrong whenever we so desire."

Eva was taken aback. She knew Tony was a closet thinker, but she hadn't often heard those thoughts. There was nothing enlightening about spreadsheets and office politics.

"I think that may have been the point. For all we know, the bird was the bad guy and the snake was defending itself. The same with the elephant and the octopus. Who's to say who did what with such a limited perspective?"

"Wow. I didn't expect that. What do you think it means?"

Tony thought for a second. "Maybe…in a black and white picture, we're supposed to see not everything is so black and white. That there are questions to ask and answers to seek before we jump to conclusions of what's right and what's wrong."

"Hmmm, and people say I'm the smart one," Eva teased as she looked at Tony with a small grin.

Knowing that her boyfriend was coming out of his shell more and more as time went on was something she always enjoyed. Back when they'd been in college, she'd heard that Tony wasn't too keen on sharing. Yet as time went on, he never failed to surprise her.

That night they had a great dinner filled with laughter. They hadn't gotten the opportunity to spend time together like this since the move. They were always having to go to work or to an engagement of some sort. Eva got more than she could ever have wished out of this birthday evening.

Even Travis, their waiter, joined in on their birthday celebration. He had heard Tony say something about it being Eva's birthday, so he brought the staff together and, as he was bringing out dessert, they sang, "Happy birthday to you. Happy birthday to you. Happy birthday dear Eva!! Happy birthday to you!"

Then they presented her with a piece of German chocolate cake with a lit candle on top. She blew it out and made a wish.

"What did you wish for?" Tony asked, hoping she would break birthday tradition and let him in on her secret wish.

"That's for me to know." She shot Tony a wink, knowing keeping him in suspense would bug him.

Once they left the restaurant, they called for a ride home, but before their car showed up, Tony noticed something out of the corner of his eye. There was an older gentleman sitting on a bench as if he was waiting for something. He wasn't homeless or anything. It looked as if the clothes he had on had been washed or were new, so he had money and a place to sleep.

"Did you guys enjoy your birthday celebration?"

Tony was caught off guard. Who was he talking to?

"Excuse me, are you talking to us?"

The strange man laughed. It was the most joyous laugh tony had ever heard. "Yes, son, I was. Don't worry I'm not stalking you. I heard singing and looked and saw you two in the window."

This made Tony even more curious.

"Oh, well thank you. And yes, we did. Thank you for asking. Are you waiting for someone? Do you need a ride?" "No, I'm okay. Sometimes I just come out here to think. Sometimes I figure out what I need to do the next day. Other times I just have retrospective time to myself."

Tony found himself becoming more and more curious about this man with the hearty laugh sitting on a sidewalk bench.

"If you don't mind me asking, what do you do for a living, sir?"

"Oh, nothing. I'm retired now. My thoughts on the next day usually have to do with in what neck of the woods I'll find myself. When I was employed, though, I was paid to clean up other peoples' messes."

"Oh, you were a janitor?"

"Tony!!" Eva said sternly.

"It's okay," The man interjected. "You could say I was a janitor of sorts. What about you, son? What ladder do you find yourself climbing?"

"I work with accounts at a private firm. What makes you think I'm climbing the ladder?"

"A young man like you, coming to a restaurant like this with his lady on her birthday instead of going out to party and drinking with the other kids your age? You must have something big in your crosshairs. Not to mention, you picked a woman with who clearly has some tact and understands social convention. I'd wager you're climbing the ladder with your firm and she is one of the only people on this planet who you want to spend time with. Am I right?"

Tony was taken aback.

His laugh was one of a happy-go-lucky retiree. His words and his tone were those of someone who had climbed a ladder of his own.

"Yes sir. I'm Tony, by the way."

The man smiled as he looked Tony in the eye and reached out his hand to offer a firm handshake.

"Jimmy. Pleased to meet you."

Tony and Eva's car pulled up, but Tony didn't want to leave Jimmy yet. For some reason he couldn't put his finger on, this enigma. He was a retiree who had cleaned for a living. Yet he clearly understood people. Why was he not doing something on a high level for a company somewhere? He just seemed like someone Tony had known all of his life; the way Tony was drawn to him.

"Well, Jimmy, I'm afraid we have to go now. It was nice meeting you. Do you find yourself on the west side of town often?"

Jimmy looked back at Tony with a smile.

"Actually, that's where I was heading tomorrow. Have you ever heard of *Ka-fe café* on that side of town?"

"Yes, I have. It's actually not that far away from me. When will you be there?"

"Whenever you're there, I suppose."

"Okay. Well, I'll be there around 7:30 a.m."

"Sounds good to me. I'll be there tomorrow at 7:30 a.m."

Tony shook his hand one more time as he said goodbye to Jimmy, got into the car and went home with Eva.

Chapter 8

After another month passed, Brittany found herself on the hot seat with her board of advisors. They didn't think it wise for Brittany to keep relying on sheer luck to continue to grow the company. They were trying to convince her to hire a marketing firm to maximize their exposure while they were on the rise.

Brittany, however, wouldn't hear of it. She was the only one in who room who knew that it wasn't luck. The advisors plead with her that this could increase their bottom line if they got more of the market share. They couldn't understand why Brittany was so combative against the idea. But she was the golden child.

Since she had taken over the company, she'd grown it considerably. When she wanted something done, she found a way to get it done, so usually the board just fell in line with whatever direction she chose to take, but they could not side with her on this. They couldn't possibly keep growing if they didn't continue to try to get better. What they didn't know, however, was that Brittany had a deal with the city's number one machine manufacturer and distributor.

So as Brittany was railing against the idea because she knew it would do more harm to the company than good, she was right. Almost every major company building in the city that was being built or renovated went through Jesse. So long as she kept dealing with Jesse, more money toward exposure would simply be an unnecessary expense.

An hour or so after the meeting, Jesse returned to her office.

"I don't think I've ever seen someone who worked so hard when she didn't have to," Jesse said, knowing their arrangement had brought most of her business in for the last year and a half. "It's almost like you're preparing to do this without me someday."

"I can't depend on you forever. One day I'm going to have to be a big girl and do all of this on my own."

"Not before you give me what you owe me, I hope. We still have an appointment to keep, my dear."

"Goodness, you're worse than my husband. You know full well that I have a lot on my plate right now. I don't know why it's so hard to get you men to realize a woman doesn't have to be your indentured servant and do everything that pleases you. I have things to do, just like you."

"That's not my problem. You wanted to play with the big dogs. Now you have to deal with the big fleas, too. Unlike your hubby, I know about our arrangement. Say other people find out how you've managed to rise to the top so quickly…well, they may not be as understanding as I am about it."

"Ha! Yeah, you have just as much skin in this game as I do. What would happen if your wife were to find out how you like to spend your long evenings away from your family?" Brittany said, not realizing who she was dealing with.

"The question you need to ask, my dear, is why would I enter into a business deal with a woman when I had absolutely nothing to gain from her partnership? Whether your company or another has their hands in the pot is of little consequence to me. My machines are going to build the skyscrapers in this city whether Brittany or Joe heads up this company."

The wheels started turning in Brittany's head as she listened to Jesse's speech.

"My children are adults now and I'm not too fond of my wife. If I were you, I wouldn't call my bluff on this one."

At that moment Brittany, realized she was in over her head. She could see in Jesse's eyes that he was dead serious. This wasn't at all what she'd thought it would be.

She was truly under his thumb. He could run her name through the mud and destroy her marriage and there was nothing she could do about it.

"Yeah. Nice try. I'll tell you what. You are right about one thing. You have helped me on a quick rise, so I should make it more of a priority to uphold my end of the bargain. Meet me at our spot in an hour and I'm all yours. Though, be warned, don't ever threaten me again or our deal is off."

That night, Brittany did as she'd said she would. Reluctantly, she went to their usual place and upheld her end of the bargain. She was bold in front of Jesse in order to save face, but she knew where this relationship was headed. Even on the way to their pied-a-terre, she began to feel ashamed.

She couldn't believe she'd let herself be put under the thumb of someone like him. Worse, she couldn't believe what she had done to her marriage. Before, it was just a means to an end. But now, with serious threats to expose their relationship to her husband, she realized she didn't want to lose Blake, but she didn't know how to get out of the situation she found herself in.

On her way home, once the deed had been done, she decided to tell Blake what she had done. One way or another, eventually he was going to find out, and it would be better if Blake found out from her. Blake was the last person in this world who cared enough about her to stick by her through all this mayhem, and all he'd gotten in return was a bitter wife. She was almost moved to tears, but she knew this was all on her and she didn't deserve to be the one crying.

Now she had to be an adult and confess to some of her darkest sins. The whole ride was filled with thoughts both of Blake showing forgiveness and compassion or him dumping her on the spot.

She didn't know if she could handle losing another loved one, but she never stopped the car. She knew she was between a rock and a hard place no matter how badly she wanted to get out. As she arrived at her abode, it was the longest walk from the car she'd ever taken in her life. Her heart was pounding, her blood was rushing, and she could practically feel the hairs standing up on the back of her neck.

"Hey, how was your day, honey?" Blake asked as she entered the house. "Hey by the way, I need a favor. I won't be able to go with the housekeeper to get the puppy tomorrow. Do you think you could take a half day and go in my place? Just for a little while until I can make it back."

"Blake, I can't. I really need to talk to you about something."

"Wait--why can't you?"

"Because I'm in the middle of very important negotiations I can't miss, you know that. But that's not the point. I really need to tell you something."

At this point, Blake was frustrated because his wife seemingly didn't want to be a part of building a life with him. "Gosh, is that job really all that matters to you? Can I get my wife to do me a favor just once? One time, please? I just need 30 minutes out of your day."

"Blake, please. Just let me talk right now. Please?"

"No, not right now. You know I try so hard just to be there and be supportive, but clearly this is a one-way street. Let me ask you something. Where did you actually go on Wednesday about a month ago? And before you try to tell me I'm seeing things--I saw the plates on the car and I know it was yours. And it was all the way on the other side of town. Since you can't make time for me, what exactly have you been making time for away from your job, gym, and yoga studio?"

"Blake can we please not do this now?" By now, Brittany was beginning to lose herself in her own thoughts. Not only did she have to confess about Jesse, but now she just remembered that there have been multiple affairs over the years that might come to light if Jesse decided to make good on his promise one day.

She began to unravel. "Please. I just really need to tell you something and I need you to listen to me."

"No, I think I've done enough listening in this relationship. Are you going to answer my question or not?"

"Blake, I'm trying to tell you there's something more important right now."

"Fine. You know what? For once I think I'll be the one who storms out. I'll pack some things to go stay somewhere else until you decide I'm important enough to you to do something as simple as get a puppy or even answer a freaking question."

Brittany was mortified. She couldn't believe Blake would resort to leaving. After all the things she had put him through, she didn't have the heart to stop him. Her dealings with Jesse for the past 12 hours had made her see what kind of men there were in this world and she suddenly realized what she had and what she'd thrown away.

She collapsed to the floor in tears, but at that point, Blake had decided enough was enough. He didn't stop. He just kept packing his things.

Brittany was now on the floor sobbing, trying her best to hold it in, but she couldn't any longer. Since her mother had died, she'd never really had enough time to deal with the loss. She was thrust into the business world and given a company before she had even read a single profit and loss statement.

"I'M HAVING AN AFFAIR!" she screamed out.

Blake stopped in in his tracks. He was in the doorway just standing…and then suddenly, he slammed the door, went into the bedroom and screamed.

Brittany could hear him in the room screaming and slamming drawers shut. All she could do was sit there, face in hands, sobbing. When Blake finally came out of the bedroom, he had two full suitcases packed as he headed full-steam for the door. He didn't even stop to look at Brittany on his way past.

As he made it to the doorway, Brittany quietly said "Just tell me you love me…please…"

Blake, again, stopped in the doorway.

He wanted to be forgiving. He wanted to turn around and say they could work on it. He wanted to be the man who stood by his wife when she needed his help the most.

Instead, he just shut the door, made his way to his car, and drove away.

There Brittany sat, thinking about all she'd been through and all she had done. It mortified her. The affairs, the hostility towards Blake, the alienation of her friends, the illegitimate business deals and the list just kept going on and on. Brittany had sank lower than the floor would allow her to go, and for the first time in her life, she knew it. This sent her into a depressive state. She suddenly lost the desire to move. She had no impetus to go clean herself up, eat, go to work, reach out to a friend or contact any human, for that matter. That night, she barely ended up making her way to the bed.

For the next week, she didn't move any farther than she had to in order to keep herself alive, which was a struggle in and of itself.

She had even thought about ending it all. She couldn't deal with the thought of what her mother would say if she knew about the woman her daughter had become.

Brittany didn't know what she wanted. All she knew was she wanted the pain to stop. Since she was a girl, she'd felt as if no one would listen to her. After what her father did with Tony, along with the tantrum she'd thrown shortly thereafter, it was as if every problem she'd tried to bring to her father had been chalked up to her just being emotional.

Her friends, while caring, had always seemed to care more about themselves. Trying to get them to have a real conversation was like trying to train a sloth to win a marathon. Her father had taken off, her mother had died, and now, through her own actions, Blake was gone. She didn't know if he would ever come back after what she had done.

Blake wouldn't return her calls, and she understood why. Whenever she did leave her place, she always hoped to see Blake or his car so she could explain herself and apologize.

But for now, she was alone.

Tony found himself in a lot more meetings since he had gotten close to the CFO. The account he had been given charge of had started doing business with them, but the minds involved with their deals knew they were holding back. There was more they had to offer.

The meetings were mainly to continue the process of ingratiating themselves with their new clients, while also waiting for any clue of what their new clients might be waiting for before they would trust Tony and his company completely.

Aside from his dealings with his new account, he and his new friend were getting along swimmingly. They typically went out for a minor meal after dealing with the representatives for Tony's new project for his clients.

Bill told Tony how impressed he was with Tony's preparation for every meeting. He never came to a meeting blind or apprehensive in any way.

"You clearly understand the importance of other people having confidence that you know what you're doing," Bill would say.

This made Tony well up with pride. All of his hard work was finally paying off, because Tony wasn't doing anything different than what he had been doing since he was a freshman in high school.

He had built in the habits of success. He was astute and detail-oriented when it came to his clients' needs, just as he'd been persistent and repetitious when it came to his studies. Tony could already see his client portfolio expanding. He knew he had room to do more, and he relished the opportunity to show of what he was capable. But first he would have to prove he could handle one account. He was well aware of this fact, which is why he never shirked his duties. It was only one account, but this account would lead to many more.

One day, after he'd left their offices for the day, he decided to grab a hot dog to eat on the way home. He was thinking about his next meeting and what he could do to help his clients achieve their goals and maybe that was the way to figure out what they were holding back.

Maybe it's the structure of the contract.

As he was putting the condiments on his hot dog, someone ran into him and he looked their direction. They didn't even break stride. They just kept walking.

"Such is the city life," mumbled Tony. He turned around to continue dressing his meal, but as he was turning, a glimmer caught his eye.

He turned in the other direction to see the person walking away. He thought he knew who it was, but he couldn't believe his eyes. He was sure, but he had to test it.

"Brittany!!" he called loudly.

She turned around and saw his face, and time stopped.

Neither of them could believe what they were seeing. It was like they were seeing ghosts, each waiting for the other to make a move or show a sign that they weren't dreaming.

But there they stood.

Tony took a step…and then Brittany took a step, afraid they might be figments of their imaginations.

They kept walking toward each other, and then Brittany reached out her hand and Tony reached out his hand to clasp hers. They gazed at each other one final time and then Tony confirmed in his heart what the glimmer was.

It was the ring he'd given her all those years ago.

He couldn't believe she had kept it all this time.

Then the two shared a hug that neither of them ever thought they would have the privilege to be a part of again. Lifted off the ground, Brittany hoped her feet never touched the ground again. After everything she had been through recently, she wished that she could stay in Tony's arms forever. Tony loved seeing Brittany again, but he knew he couldn't spend the rest of his life with her in his arms. He had Eva to think about, as well.

He put her down, looked her right in the eye and said, "I can't believe you kept that ring all this time."

To which Brittany replied, "I can't believe you remembered it for all these years."

"Gosh, look at you. You've grown up to be such a beautiful woman."

Brittany let out a quiet chuckle and a smirk and said, "Yeah, maybe on the outside."

Tony couldn't believe what he was hearing. The Brittany he'd always known was so sweet.

"What do you mean? Is that why you look like you're about to cry? Tell me what's wrong?"

"My mom is dead, Tony. I got married and had a series of affairs that I think ruined my marriage, and, yes, I am married now."

Tony's eyes widened slightly, but he wasn't about to abandon Brittany after finally reconnecting with her after all this time.

"Well, don't stop there. I'm sure there's more to the story than that."

Brittany, so shocked that someone could hear all of that and still stick around, didn't know if she should continue telling the story. As far as she was concerned, they had already gotten past the hardest part. What more damage could be done, right?

She decided to tell Tony about her descent from grace.

"I don't think I have time to tell you the whole story, but I can give you a synopsis."

"Okay, I have time."

Brittany could barely believe what she was hearing. The friends she'd had in her life up to that point would have interrupted her when she'd wanted to vent or would have told her she was just stressed.

Here goes nothing, Brittany thought to herself.

"A few years back, my mom died. And to make matters worse, it was on my wedding day. I stayed in my room and cried and cried for hours--days, actually. If it wasn't for Blake, I don't think I ever would have left that room, even for graduation, where I got a standing ovation and so much support from the student body. After graduation, I got a letter from my father and a key, essentially saying the company was mine. The key was just a symbol that he'd sent with the letter, though. Then I found myself wondering why he would do this now? He may have lost his wife, but I'd lost my mother, too…"

Brittany remembered the flood of emotions she'd had when she'd read the letter and it began to spill out while she was talking to Tony. She shed a few tears before she pulled herself together and continued her story.

"So, I decided later that day that instead of finding him and pulling him out of whatever hole into which he was planning to retreat, that I would take him up on his offer. Not only would I run the company, but I would run it better than he ever could. As far as I was concerned, I made the best grades at a school that had given me the finest education in the nation. As I stop and think about it now, maybe the same thing crossed his mind, which is why he thought I was ready to take such a big jump. It doesn't matter, though. Regardless of whether or not that was the case, it was still selfish on his part."

Brittany put her hands over her face, trying not to break down with the added stress of how much she still blamed her father for ruining her life at every stage. Every time he had an opportunity to make a decision, he made the wrong one, as far as Brittany was concerned.

"Then I found myself sitting in a room with all of these businessmen looking at me with such…*contempt*. The way they were leering at me let me know that they all thought I shouldn't be there. But just like with my dad, I didn't back down. I decided I could prove them wrong, as well. In the following months, we had a lot of proposals, bids and deals my father had been working on before he left, and we didn't get a single one of them.

"Months of working late hours and busting my butt trying to learn on the fly what my father had been building for the last 20 years, and I had fallen flat on my face. I couldn't believe I couldn't close a single deal this coward of a man had facilitated. How could he do this, and I couldn't? Was there a business trick no one had ever taught me? Sometimes I'd pick up the phone and think about finding him, but I just…I just…"

Tony sensed she was headed for another breakdown and put his arm around her shoulder.

"Hey. Hey. It's okay. You don't have to tell me everything if you don't want to. I can see this is tearing you up bit by bit."

"It's okay. I want to tell you. But thank you. So, after months of failures, I started noticing that almost all the machines that were doing construction in the city had the same symbol on them. So, I requested an audience with their owner. I figured I could form an alliance with him, just owner-to-owner conversation, you know?

"When I got to his office, he wasn't what I expected at all. He looked down on me like my advisors did. He asked me so many questions that I didn't have answers to and he just kept moving closer and closer to me as he was asking. Then, at the end of the questions, he asked, 'Why should I? What's in it for me?' That's when I realized he was right. I didn't have an answer to any of his questions. I had no business in his office. I also knew this partnership might be my only shot at saving my spot at the head of the company. I knew I would have to give the board something soon or they would take legal action and try to get me removed. So, I began to rub his chest, and you know what comes next.

"Afterward, I told him he could expect that every time he helped me to close a deal. He eventually agreed. Then, when I went home to see Blake, he just kept telling me how he wished I'd sell the company because it was stressing me out so much. He just kept going on and on about it, and that night I had basically just sold my soul to keep it. I looked at him and realized what I'd done never even crossed his mind, but I felt guilty.

"The guilt I felt just made matters worse, until I finally got defensive. I started to push him away. I got my first deal, and then a second and third. On the fourth, I met a man who just made me feel like I wasn't out of place. That I could hold my own and I didn't need to be babied. I began having an affair with him which ended soon thereafter.

"Over the next six-to-eight months or so, multiple affairs started and ended. The only two that persisted were with the businessman and another guy I'd met later.

"And, of course, it all blew up in my face later, when the machine tycoon and I had a disagreement. In his defense, I wasn't holding up my end of our arrangement. After a good span of time avoiding him, he finally showed up and threatened to expose our affair if I didn't uphold my end of our agreement. So, I did. The problem was that afterward, I realized I was truly under this man's thumb and I didn't want to live like that.

"Then I realized I'd have to tell Blake about the affair. And then I realized it wasn't just one affair. All at once it hit me. The things I'd done over the past year or so just to win the approval of a man who had spent my whole life seemingly trying to prove to me I was an idiot. That I'll probably never even see again. When I finally got home, I had every intention of just coming out and telling Blake about the affair, but he was already done at that point.

"He was packing his bags and leaving before I even told him about the affair. I didn't get to get to that part until he was basically out of the door. Of course, me telling him that didn't help anything. Aaaand that's why it looks like I'm about to cry. Because that's all I've been doing since he left."

Tony was sitting straightforward with his hands clasped as he listened to her. He wasn't looking at her. Just listening to her tell her story. The whole time she was talking, he never flinched. He never moved closer or farther away. He just sat as if he was in a trance, seeing something no one else could see. For a while, Brittany stared at him, wondering what was going through his mind. She didn't know who this new man might be--if it was still her long-lost friend or if he would condemn her.

"I think…"

Brittany began to sink, knowing what Tony was going to say.

"I think…you should go home and get some rest."

Brittany opened her eyes, looked at Tony and began to cry.

"What? Why?"

"I think you've done the best anyone could have asked of you. You were in an impossible situation where thousands if not millions of people would have cracked and died under the pressure, but you held it together. I'm not saying anything you did was right, but that's something you'll have to atone for in your own way. One thing I do know is there are people in this world who don't get the puppy they wanted and they become sadistic and destructive.

"The only person you put in harm's way was yourself. You're still in there somewhere. I think you should just go home and get some rest and grieve. The world never gave you a chance to lose your mother and best friend. You should take that time now."

Brittany could not believe her ears. If she'd told that story to anyone else, they would have told her how she was a horrible person, or that she deserved for Blake to leave her. They would have said she was in the wrong and she had no right to cry over any of this because she'd brought it on herself. Yet here Tony was, acting calm, as if he hadn't heard a word she'd said.

"Did you hear everything I just told you?"

"I heard every word. You've beaten yourself up enough. You know what you did wasn't right. Why should I make any of this worse for you? To be honest, Brittany, this is going to sound weird, but I am so proud of you. I mean, people lose their parents and become recluses for months. You lost your mother and father and inherited a company. You didn't pick up a drug habit, you didn't become abusive and you didn't drag anyone else down with you.

"That says a lot. Of course, you still have to answer to Blake for all you've done, but dang, I think even I would have lost my mind if I was put in your shoes."

Brittany stared at Tony.

"What?" Tony thought maybe he had said something wrong.

Then Brittany gave him another big hug, which jolted Tony. He hadn't seen that coming at all, and quite frankly, he didn't even know why she was hugging him again.

"Okay, I missed you too," Tony said nervously.

"I'm sorry," Brittany said as she tried to wipe the tears from her face. "I just really needed to hear that."

Tony became curious. "So what's next?"

"I don't know…honestly, after everything I've done, If Blake never speaks to me again, I wouldn't blame him. But I want to make things right between us and I just don't know how. Tony, I only told him about one affair. What will he do when he finds out about the others?"

"What do you think he'll do?"

"Recent history suggests that he'll leave."

"Do you think that has to be the only outcome?"

"No, but why would he stay with me?"

"I wish I could tell you, I really do, but I think you will be doing Blake a disservice if you don't tell him everything and let him decide for himself."

"So how should I tell him?"

"Just be honest. Don't overthink it or dance around the truth. If he leaves, then that's his choice, and it will hurt. But for all we know he still loves you and wants to be with you."

Brittany stopped and thought about Tony's words for a second.

"Would you still want to be with me after what I've done?"

Tony thought hard on the situation. "Honestly, I don't know. I don't know what your relationship has been like aside from the infidelity. I don't know if he's had any affairs of his own. Heck, I don't even pretend to know what you two have been through together since you met. I guess I'd say it all depends on whether I thought the pain was worth it or not. But to be honest, it would probably be a 50/50 chance at this point."

Brittany looked at Tony once again with nostalgia. She couldn't believe the kind of man he had become. She could tell he was still a thinker, as he'd always been. Certainly he was just as unpredictable, sweet and honest. She sat there looking at him…wondering…

"I think I'll take your advice now."

"What? What advice?"

"I think I'll go home and get some rest."

"Oh, yeah, that's right. Hey, let's exchange numbers. If you need anything just send me a text or call me. I'm here for you, okay?"

"I know you are. Trust me, I'm so grateful to have you in my life. I promise I'll do my best to find the Brittany that my mom…and you…see in me."

Tony and Brittany shared a hug that lasted longer than either of them expected.

They finally separated and Tony said, "Gosh! I should get back. My girlfriend is probably wondering where I am right now."

"You have a girlfriend? You didn't mention that part," Brittany said, laughing.

"Yeah, I was kind of busy being worried about my best friend. I'll tell you all about Eva later, I promise," Tony yelled as he started to jog in the other direction.

As Tony drove home, he thought about Brittany. He couldn't believe how far apart their lives had gotten. He thought about everything she'd told him.

Maybe it's just an interesting coincidence that I saw her on this night, of all the nights I could have run into her.

Then he began to think about Eva. He remembered he'd told her he went to *Shakespeare in the Park* with a *friend*. Now that the friend in question was seemingly back in his life, Eva deserved to know who that friend was, and who she was to him. Also, on the drive home, he found himself hoping Eva wouldn't be too upset with him.

When he finally got home, he took his own advice. After he and Eva exchanged pleasantries, he told her. He told her who he had been with that night, who she was to him, and what Brittany had told him earlier. Eva, like Tony, just sat and listened to Tony's condensed version of Brittany's story.

When Tony was finally finished, she asked, "So do you think you'll see her again?"

Tony didn't know how to respond. He wasn't going to leave Eva for Brittany, but he knew that from Eva's point of view, this wasn't exactly ideal.

"Honestly, I don't know. She could fall off the map today just like her dad did, for all I know. I offered to help her because she was a friend, and I don't think she has anyone else in her life right now since her dad ran out on her."

Eva sat calmly listening to Tony and thinking about how she felt about the situation. She didn't like that someone Tony had been so close to had just magically popped back into his life after a series of affairs. Though, at the same time, Tony wasn't an idiot. If he believed she wasn't coming onto him, then the only other alternative was that Tony truly thought he could help her.

"Well, I trust you to do the right thing. I believe you really think you can help this woman. I'm not particularly happy that the two of you have the past you do, but I do trust you. BUT! Please don't hold back anything like that from me again. I want to believe you just want to help this woman, but when you hold back who she was from me like that, what else am I supposed to think besides that you still have feelings for her? However, I promise I will trust you on two conditions."

"Okay, whatever you want."

"You never, ever, go anywhere alone with her without telling me first."

"I promise."

"And two, you have to promise you have no feelings for her and you'll never cheat on me with her."

"You have my word," "Tony said as he kissed her.

Chapter 9

The next day, it was time for Tony's weekly meeting with Jimmy and he knew exactly what he wanted to talk about. In the past, Tony and Jimmy had a very good relationship. In the beginning, when they started meeting at the coffee shop, Tony was just curious about the man. He'd wanted to figure out what gave him that jolly laugh and what a brilliant man like Jimmy was doing sitting on a bench outside of a restaurant. However, as time went on, he came more for Jimmy's perspective on life than anything.

They talked about everything from business to the evolution of sports. Jimmy was a nice man, which was probably why everything he said sounded just a little naïve. But Tony didn't mind. He preferred Jimmy's naivety to the cynicism he heard from some of his coworkers. Soon, Jimmy became a sounding board for Tony when it came to ideas, his relationship with Eva and even what he'd heard in a business meeting that might have thrown him a bit for a loop.

Tony didn't always heed what Jimmy said, but it was nice to have the perspectives from both sides before he made a major decision. One of the main reasons Tony kept meeting him was something Jimmy had told him about friendships. It helped Tony recognize all the negative talk his co-workers were putting in his ear about handling an account that big without having any experience. They always told Tony they were joking, but it kept happening again and again until Jimmy suggested maybe they weren't real friends.

He'd said, "Real friends shouldn't have to put each other down just to have a conversation. Envying your rise is normal. It's not right, but it's normal. Almost everyone you meet will be trying to advance in one thing or another.

"The difference in situations with negative friends, however, is they're usually envious because you have outgrowing them. They could have put in the same work as you and learned the business just as well as you had. They had the same coworkers, had access to the same information, had the same proximity to each other, etc. Yet none of them did what you did. Now they blame you for working hard without them. You do your best to forgive these people…but that doesn't mean you should have to compromise your standards to do so."

So for Tony, this was another opportunity to gain perspective from a man he had grown to respect. When they sat down for coffee, Tony was so nervous he couldn't help himself.

"I ran into an old friend last night," he exclaimed.

Jimmy was so startled he sat bolt upright in his seat.

"Okay. I run into friends all the time. What makes this particular one so special to you?"

"Well, I grew up with her. I spent days at the park with her. I was there when she got sick from eating sand out of the sand box and she was there when I cut my forearm open on a nail. We've been through so much together. I remember once when we were kids, we were hopping a fence to get into a playground for kids with their parents. Our parents were at work, of course, but it wasn't like anyone checked with the kids and asked where their parents were. I didn't really want to do it, but I also wanted to be with Brittany, so I went. She knew I could chicken out at any point, so she made me go over the fence first. After I got over, I waited for her to get over, but she didn't jump far enough and caught her pants on the fence. They ripped horribly on the backside to where her underwear were showing.

I was laughing so hard that it didn't even register to go look for help. She was so mad she didn't talk to me for a week," Tony said, chuckling. He didn't realize it, but for a second, Jimmy caught him staring off into space. He could tell Tony was going down memory lane. Jimmy stared back at him, smirking.

Tony looked at him and said, "What? Did I say something wrong?"

"No. So this woman. You were in love with her as a kid, weren't you?"

"What!?!? I just told you we were friends. What would make you think I was in love with her?"

"Son, there aren't too many things in this world a man focuses on.

"Most of the time it can be boiled down to two things. At first, that thing is… himself. What he wants, who he wants, how he can get it and where it might be. No matter how idiotic or destructive he is, when a young man has his eye on something, if he wants it bad enough, he'll find a way to get it."

"I can't argue with you there. What's the second thing?"

Jimmy appeared to be waiting for Tony to come up with the answer himself. Then, he said, "His heart."

"His heart? Aren't men the non-emotional of the two genders?"

Jimmy let out one of his classic laughs and said, "Really?? So you think men have a higher suicide rate than women because…we just like the taste of bullets? Or do men end up making knee-jerk emotional decisions because we're always fighting to hold up an appearance and therefore never deal with our emotions until it's too late? Those men are just heartbroken, Tony. Not able to take care of their family the way they want, live the life they want, get the woman they want, or else they lose something they love. They aren't as selfish as most think. I truly believe they just want the pain to stop. That, my friend, is a clear sign of a heart which feared the light of the world so much that it would rather die in its cage than let someone come in and help."

Tony couldn't believe what he was hearing. He couldn't figure out if Jimmy was speaking from experience or he'd just lived a lot of life. Either way, none of what Jimmy was saying had ever crossed his mind before. For a second, he drifted off in admiration of this strange man, but then he came back into the conversation and said, "So you're saying I was in love with her whether I knew it or not?"

Tony said. Still trying to deny the obvious.

"That's for you to decide. I'm just here for the coffee."

Tony laughed a little at Jimmy's nonchalance. "Come on, Jimmy. You can't just say something like that and leave me hanging!"

To which Jimmy responded, "The problem I think you might be having, in my humble opinion, is you think there's only one way to love someone. Which most people do, so it's not horrible."

"What do you mean by that?"

"Well, everyone always wants to put love in a box, because we find ourselves putting everything in a box. Who's dangerous? Who looks like they'll be nice? Who raises their children this way? Are they or are they not a good person based off of things that, quite frankly, have nothing to do with their character? Sure, it's a great survival mechanism for most things. I'm not telling you to give the keys to your car to an active car thief. But when it comes to matters of people's hearts, that's another story entirely."

"So, you don't think there's any way to be able to know someone's intentions by their actions?"

Jimmy paused for a few seconds in deep thought. Then he replied, "Tell me--which parent loves their child more? The parent who sends their child to time-out or the parent who spanks their child? Which husband loves his wife more? The husband who is doing all he can to make ends meet and comes home with a bouquet of flowers, or the rich man who takes his wife to her favorite five-star restaurant once a month? Who's better? Who's right and who's wrong? See, Tony, I believe the problem you're having right now is you, like most, believe if you still love her that you must leave Eva, at least to a certain extent.

"I'm telling you that sometimes the best way to love someone is to leave them alone. Show them more attention. Show them less attention. Give them more gifts or give them less gifts. It's all subjective. The only thing you can control is the heart behind the action."

At this point, Tony was confused. "But listen. She came back into my life last night, and basically told me her life has been torn apart. The thing is, I want to help, but is it wrong since I have Eva?"

"You're not listening, son. I'm telling you that you might just love your old friend in a different way. Most people inherently think *different* means *wrong*. Even worse, most people think *emotion* equals *attachment*. That's how we end up in if/then relationships."

"If/then relationships?" Tony asked.

"Yes. IF you like what I like THEN I'll be your friend. IF you believe what I believe in THEN I'll help you. And that's not love. Do you think any mother worth her salt has ever uttered the words, 'IF my child learns how to walk THEN I'll raise him? No. Because a mother's love for her child is unconditional. That's true love.

"What you're feeling for your friend right now is the wrong kind of love. You're busy thinking this is between Eva and Brittany when your mind should be made up."

"Made up how?"

"Eva should never have to compete with Brittany. Point blank, period. Eva is first. Brittany, on the other hand--help her the best you can, but if you can't help her, then you just can't help her."

Tony was deep in thought, wondering what Jimmy was trying to tell him, and if his interpretation of Jimmy's message was what he'd intended. More so than this, he wondered if his interpretation of Jimmy's word was correct.

Was Jimmy right?

"So it's really that simple, huh?"

"Tony, let me give you some advice that people should give more often. You could lose."

"To be honest, that doesn't sound like great advice."

"Of course not. That's why this conundrum is bothering you so much. Tony, sometimes in life you've done all you can. You come early, stay late, study extra hard, eat right, attend all the meetings, and you can still lose. I'm telling you that you can pay for her to have a room in a psych ward, pay her rent, introduce her to better friends, help her get a job and she can still make the same mistakes again. Now, does that mean you should never help another human ever again? Of course not! All it means is you lost THIS TIME, but that's all it was. It doesn't mean you don't try again. In most cases, you have to learn from your past and try again before something will work."

Tony and Jimmy had mutual respect between them. It was like they had known each other all of their lives. Tony hung on Jimmy's every word.

Jimmy noticed and admired Tony's willingness to learn from someone who'd been a complete stranger not so long ago. He didn't know what was in store for Tony, but he knew he had a bright future ahead of him.

Brittany had gone back to her place after she had seen Tony. Afterward, for the next week or so, she spent most of her time in deep thought. At first, her thoughts mainly revolved around what a horrible person she had become and how she had lost the one person on this planet who still cared about her. There was something inside of her mind she couldn't get to, an itch she just couldn't scratch.

How did this happen? Why didn't I just sell?

Every way she could attack herself, she did so with precision. Every minor detail of her darkest secrets were brought to life for judgement, but it didn't help. She still found herself wondering if she would get Blake back. Worse, she wondered if she even deserved the forgiveness needed for them to be together again.

Thankfully, she'd run into Tony. She hadn't realized it at first, but he'd helped her tremendously. For the first time since Blake had left, she honestly felt as if there might be a slight glimmer of hope. However, this still left the major problem of how she could convince him she could do better. That she could *be* better. Like Tony had said, she had to let Blake make his choice, and when the time came, she wanted to help him see she had changed. Then she thought of the fact that she'd only told Blake about one affair.

What if I tell him about the others?" she would think to herself. Should I even tell him about the others? I mean, once you've had one affair, a few more isn't that much worse, right?

In her eyes, it couldn't get any worse. This wasn't a decision for her to make, however. She knew she had to talk to Tony again. The last time they'd met, her reminiscence almost overcame her.

Towards the end of their last conversation she'd started thinking about all the good times they'd had. One time in particular, when they were kids, they had been playing cops and robbers in the house. Brittany had been looking back at Tony, who was chasing her and trying to catch her, which he never could. In the one moment she didn't look where she was going, she'd ended up knocking over a very expensive vase Tony's mother had gotten on an overseas trip. Brittany had cried and cried, knowing she was going to get into trouble. Their parents had warned them not to run in the house. When Tony's parents came in and saw what happened, Tony spoke up and claimed he'd been the one who broke the vase because they were running through the house and he wasn't looking where he was going.

Brittany also thought about the time Tony had asked if she would be his girlfriend and had pulled a ring out of his pocket. She'd thought about the weeks that followed. At that moment, she felt like that might have been the best time of her life.

Now, all she wanted was Blake back in her life. She knew it was risky, but Tony was the only person she felt like she could talk to. No one else understood her the way Tony did, and he hadn't looked at her with disgust when she'd confessed and confided in him the other night. So she decided to send Tony a text asking if she could meet him again.

Tony replied that he would have to check with Eva first. Then Brittany assured him it would be in a public place. Moments later, after clearing it with Eva, Tony agreed to the meeting. When they met up, Brittany was happy. At first she went to hug Tony, but then she drew back.

Tony was confused. "What's wrong?"

"I don't know if I should hug you or not."

Tony smiled. "It's okay. I told Eva all about you. She knows why I'm here. It's okay if you hug me. Not now, though. Now it would just be weird."

Brittany burst into laughter before she clapped a hand over her mouth in embarrassment. It was the first time she had laughed like that since Blake had left.

Tony motioned for Brittany to have a seat and then asked, "So what's on your mind?"

Brittany didn't know how to broach the subject with Tony. It was a sensitive subject and she knew Tony might not have good news for her.

She decided to just come out and say what was on her mind. "I want to show Blake that I've changed. I just don't know how. I don't know if I should call my former lovers and tell them it's over. I want to be able to go to work and not feel like I have to look over my shoulder and see a piece of the past few years rearing its ugly head. I want to be a nicer person to people, but I don't know how. It just seems like so much. I'm overwhelmed. What should I do?"

Tony leaned back in his chair as he listened to Brittany.

His eyes went wide with surprise at how fast all of what Brittany said came out.

"Well…" Tony pushed his fingers back through is hair, wondering how he should respond, trying to figure out what he would do it if he were in Brittany's position. "Honestly, I'm not going to lie to you, I have no idea."

Brittany was shocked. "Really? I can't say I expected that response."

Tony quickly responded, "I mean…it's not that I don't want to say anything. I just haven't been in that situation before. I haven't even known anyone who's been in your situation."

Tony paused before saying, "If I were in your position, I would try honesty."

"Honesty?"

"Yeah, I mean, you can't control what Blake does or what people think about you. All you can really do at this point is be authentic. This isn't something which will just go away with a simple apology. I feel whomever you decide to apologize to may not believe if you just *say* you're sorry and leave it at that. But if they see that you've changed, then there's nothing else you can do besides show them.

"It has to be honest and authentic, though. I've heard a lot of stories at work and I've heard them apologize to each other sometimes. It's always an act and everyone can tell it's not the truth. The point of an apology is to show contrition, which can't be the case if you still feel as if you have ground to stand on or they absolutely should apologize to you, too. An apology has to be shown with no expectation of anything in return."

"What do you mean ground to stand on? Like if I felt justified or something?"

"Actually, yes. That, too. I didn't even think about it. I was saying that, for example, when I mess up really bad with Eva--like sell her jewelry bad…long story, a college garage sale gone wrong. Anyway, I always feel as if I'm sinking in guilt until I apologize and have her forgive me to be pulled out of it. That's how I feel when I'm seeking her forgiveness. I was wrong and that's that. At least that's what my mother used to tell me when I would take the rap for something Jeremy did at school.

"Ninety-nine times out of 100, Jeremy did it and I was just covering for him if it was something minor. The sentiment is still the same, though, I think. Try telling Blake the truth and letting him make the choice himself. That's all you can really do at this point."

Brittany was listening to Tony's every word. She heard him, but he said one thing she hoped he didn't mean without even realizing it--that she should tell Blake about the other affairs.

"I mean, that makes sense, but sometimes the whole truth is too much for people, isn't it?"

"Oh, absolutely. Don't get me wrong. I'm not saying you have to detail and catalog every single thing you've done and put it on the table in front of him. With most people, you can probably get away with less. You probably didn't do much to them except be a bad person. Blake, though--he's already mad. If you think you can hide the other affairs from him for the rest of your life, then I'm not going to tell him. But if there's the slightest chance he could find out, this could all blow up in your face all over again on the off chance he doesn't file for divorce soon."

"Wow, I hadn't really thought of that. I guess I have to tell him."

"That's your choice." Brittany put her face in her hands for a while and then said, "I really don't want to, though. I know he's going to be so mad. It's just going to make everything worse."

"Well, they do dig a hole in the ground before they begin construction on a major building."

Brittany looked up at Tony with a blank stare. "That didn't help at all! The building was already built, and I took a hurricane to it," she said sarcastically.

"Hey, I'm doing my best here, okay? Don't judge me."

They both started to laugh again.

"I'm really glad I ran into you at that hotdog stand. You're still the one friend I can always count on," Brittany said as she looked off into the distance.

"I hope I can live up to those high expectations," Tony said sarcastically.

Brittany shot him a look for a second. Then they sat there for a while talking about memories from their childhood. Surprisingly, Tony remembered a lot more than Brittany thought he would. She'd thought that Tony had left her in the past a long time ago, but he still remembered everything as vividly as she did. Then they talked about their jobs for a while.

Tony still couldn't believe that Brittany's dad just up and gave her an entire company to run when Brittany had never even had a full-time job. It was truly mind-blowing. He started reminiscing and thinking about who Brittany's dad was when they'd known each other. He'd been so protective of Brittany. Why would he just throw her to the sharks like that with no training or briefing whatsoever?

Brittany was impressed with how quickly Tony was climbing the corporate ladder. As a company owner herself, she knew she wouldn't just pick some random guy out of a hat and put him in a room with Jesse or any of her other clients and expect them to be able to keep up with the conversation. They went back and forth with each other for more than an hour as if they were trying to make up for all of the years they had lost being apart from each other.

However, Brittany knew that it had to come to an end eventually. She would have to go and face her demons once she left.

"I think I need to go and call Blake."

"Really? Right now? Are you sure?"

"Yeah. If I don't do it now, I don't think I'll have the courage to do it later."

"Well, I can't argue with that. If you do decide to go through with it, I'm sure it's going to be tough."

"Hey, it's all about showing contrition, right?" Brittany said as she stood up. "Thank you for coming and listening to me vent."

"Anytime," Tony said, as they shared a hug. "Good luck. I hope everything turns out well."

Brittany turned and walked away, taking out her phone to make a call.

Just at that moment, Tony's phone started ringing.

"Hey, what's up?"

"Wow, that's all the greeting you give to your friends? I should have taught you some manners when we were in college."

Tony laughed and said, "Okay, hello Jeremy. How are you doing?"

"If you must know, I actually need a favor from you."

"What kind of favor?"

Jeremy proceeded to tell him what he had been into since he had been expelled from college, which Tony didn't find surprising. However, he did feel a tremendous amount of disappointment. Jeremy had been doing so well when he was in college. He feared his friend would backslide a little, but it now appeared it was worse than he'd imagined. Especially since the last time Tony had seen him, he'd made it sound like everything was better than ever.

"Who runs up a bar tab that high?!?!"

Chapter 10

As usual, on her way home, Brittany was in her head, thinking about the best way to be honest with Blake while showing him she regretted the decisions she'd made in the past. She thought about the situation as much as she could, but there was no scenario where Blake wouldn't be tremendously upset.

When she finally made it home, Blake was already there.

"What did you want to talk to me about?"

Brittany was taken back. She hadn't expected Blake to be so upset the moment as she walked through the door, but she was still determined to try to make this as painless as possible.

"How have you been?"

Blake was torn. On one hand, he knew Brittany was trying to be nice, but he just couldn't forget what he'd heard in the doorway that night. He contemplated that she might be trying to apologize to him. His nature wasn't to be mean to anyone. He just couldn't understand how he could do so much and be so patient and, as a reward, his wife had an affair behind his back. An affair of which he still didn't know the details. *How long had it been going on? Was it a mutual friend? Did he know the guy?* Blake needed answers that he didn't necessarily want.

"Brittany, I don't have time right now to mess around with this. What did you want to say to me?"

"Okay, so I was talking to a friend."

"Wait. What? What friend?"

"Just hear me out. He's an old friend of mine I knew when I was younger. I ran into him on the street one night not too long ago."

As Brittany was talking, Blake turned his head away in disgust.

As he shook his head and turned for the door, Brittany pleaded, "Blake, wait! Nothing happened between us, I swear! He is helping me to try and save us."

Blake was still upset. "So you decided to ask some other guy to help with our marriage?"

"Well, you wouldn't answer my calls or my texts. Blake, I couldn't talk to you and I didn't know what else to do. I swear I just ran into Tony one night and I started talking to him. I didn't go out looking for some random guy. It just happened."

"Oh, I guess that's what you were going to tell me about the affair, too, right? It just happened?"

Brittany was shaking with fear, but she knew the only way to get through this was to speak up. It was now or never. Blake was already halfway out of the door. She started to cry just thinking about it.

"Oh, God, I knew it there was something with that guy Tony," Blake snarled.

"No…but there were others."

"What?!?! Others?! Plural?"

"There was more than one affair. It's been going on for years now." Brittany almost collapsed as she stood there waiting for Blake to say something.

Blake glared at her, rage turning his face red.

She stood waiting for him to say something.

To lash out and break something,

Anything.

And then, she saw a tear roll down his cheek before he quickly wiped it away. Then another dropped down the other side. With tear-filled eyes, he walked away. He didn't say a word, but his message was clear. She had hurt him in a way she couldn't even imagine.

Now *she* was crying. Not because he'd left, but because she knew that what she had done Blake might never forgive. As Brittany curled up on her couch, she started to think that maybe he shouldn't. She didn't know how to stop the tears. In her mind, she knew this it was her fault and she had to have faith that Blake would forgive her.

She knew she had no right to cry after all she had done, but inside she wondered if she was hurting just as much as Blake was.

I have to get up. Blake is the one who should be hurt here, not me.

She tried everything to stop herself from feeling sorry for herself. Nothing worked. So, there she sat, with tear-filled eyes, just as Blake had. Then she realized all she was feeling was a tremendous amount of guilt. She wasn't hurt--she was ashamed. But she knew she wasn't done yet. She reached over and found her phone and dialed one of her contacts.

"Yes, ma'am?" said the voice over the phone.

"I have a favor to ask if you're up for it…"

Later, after he had thought long and hard, Tony decided to give in to Jeremy's request, so, he drove to the outskirts of town to meet him. When he got there, Jeremy was sitting on top of his car waiting for Tony.

Tony got out of the car with an envelope, handed it to Jeremy and said, "Here's the loan you needed."

"Oh, thanks man. You're a lifesaver, I knew I could count on you!"

"Actually, you can't. This is the last time I'm giving you a loan like this. I hope this helps you take care of it."

Jeremy was looking Tony eye-to-eye in surprise. After a few seconds he realized Tony was serious, so he gripped the envelope in his hand and began to walk away.

"Wait! How do you even run bar tabs up that high? What happened to you, man? You were doing so good."

Jeremy stopped, turned around and stared at Tony again. "Honestly, when I got kicked out of college, I had every intention of coming back. I would think about what you said about it only being one semester. Even when I got a job, I would remind myself it was only temporary. Then our district manager came by one day and our store manager was having trouble with our batching paperwork and a LOT of our billing. I happened to be there and remembered something we had studied in college. I told them a simple way to fix the batching and how to slowly start to correct the billing.

"Then the District manager pulled me to the side and asked me where I got my ideas from and I told him I'd been to college. He asked why I was working at their storefront and I told him I'd had to move back for family concerns. He asked for a copy of my transcript for some reason and then basically fired our manager on the spot and gave me the job. After that, I had the store for around nine months before we were audited again, and I brought the score down a little less than 70 points. Then they started sending me to a few more stores in the area to do the same thing. After a while, that became my job. The better I did, the more other higher ups started taking notice. They would invite me out for drinks, which was harmless at first.

We went out every so often and they would buy me drinks. Soon enough, I found myself out more nights than not."

As Jeremy spoke, it finally occurred to him that maybe he hadn't realized exactly how bad it had gotten up until this moment.

"You know as I say all this, I guess I should have realized a long time ago that I had a problem. The guys I was hanging out with loved it, so much so that eventually I was offered another promotion. I was the life of their parties. Most of them were middle-aged to old married guys, so they couldn't really go home too drunk. I guess they lived vicariously through me."

Jeremy shook his head and let out a little chuckle before continuing with his story. "My new job ended up being way harder than the other. Before, it was just simple paperwork and accounting issues, but now I was playing a bigger game. I didn't know if I could do it. I started thinking about what would happen if I were to fail and if I didn't excel at this job like the last. Not long afterward, I realized a quick drink usually calmed my nerves a bit and I was able to do better at work. So it became pretty common for me to be happy at happy hour.

"One thing led to another and before I knew it, I had a routine. At the apex of my habit, I was just happy that I was a regular at a lot of places and they would let me have a tab--as long as I came in and paid it every so often. Until one day I wasn't paying them. You can guess the rest, and now we're here. Honestly, if I've learned one thing through this whole thing, it's to never take something else or make a move just because someone else says that you should."

Try as he might to be stern, Tony couldn't help but start to feel sorry for his old friend. On his way to see Jeremy, he'd still been contemplating whether he should give Jeremy the loan or not. He thought about what would be best for Jeremy. On one hand, he really was in trouble financially and he wanted Jeremy to be able to get that money off his back. But Tony also wondered if he was enabling Jeremy.

How did he get himself into this mess in the first place? I knew it! I knew he didn't learn a darn thing. I just knew he was going to move back home and fall in with the wrong crowd. No. Heck, no. I shouldn't even give him the loan. He'll just go off and keep being the same knucklehead who got kicked out of college for stuff just like this.

In his heart, though, Tony wasn't capable of turning his back on a friend, no matter how much he thought he should. He went back and forth in his mind the whole way there.

So, when Jeremy said, "Well, anyway, I understand. I'll just…" and then gripped the envelope and walked away, Tony was hurt, too.

It wasn't in his nature to abandon a friend. But he didn't know how else to help him at that point. So Tony watched Jeremy get into his car and drive away, wondering if he had done the right thing.

For now, Tony couldn't focus on that. He had a big day tomorrow. After a considerable number of meetings and lunches with his new clients, along with Bill, it was finally time to close on their deal. After sitting in meetings with Bill, taking a considerable amount of notes and finding a new level of cooperation from the clients, thanks to a tip from Jimmy, Tony was ready to finalize a deal. Tony would handle the bulk of the load, but thankfully Bill wasn't unreasonable. He knew Tony had never done business on that level before. He assured Tony he would take care of the details to which Tony wasn't privy. Tony agreed. Bill had been there for him every step of the way. He was a great mentor for Tony, and Tony knew he was lucky to have him.

When the day came and they were in the meeting room across from their clients, Tony was excited. He had never dreamed he would be in this position this early in his career.

"Hello, gentlemen," Bill said, as they all shook hands, exchanged pleasantries and sat down. "Let's get right to it. We're glad you and your company find this deal agreeable. I'm assuming you had your people look it over and everything looked good on your end?"

"Yes. I can't lie. I didn't think we could get this done before the negotiations started, but I have to say, you and your protégé make a great team. I'm glad we could get this done," the client said.

The transition was seamless on their end, and the compliment they paid Bill and Tony made him look at Tony with pride.

"I think you will see this kid for a long time, even after I'm gone," Bill said.

Now the time to close the deal was finally here. All parties had copies of the proposal in front of them.

"Okay. Let's rock-and-roll with this thing, shall we?" Tony and their representative pulled out their pens and proceeded to start to sign the contracts, until Tony noticed one of the numbers and clauses hadn't been in the initial proposal he had talked about with Bill.

He stopped signing. The more he stared at it, the less sense it made.

"What's wrong, Tony?" Bill asked.

"Well, sir, I was reading the last few pages of the deal. I think there's been a mistake. I'm sorry. I think I'll have to take this home and revise it one more time before we can finalize it," Tony said as he looked at his clients. "I want you guys to get the best deal we can possibly give you. Let me take this home and look over it one more time and then I promise we'll be able to meet back here the same time tomorrow and get it done."

His clients looked at him in bewilderment, apparently waiting for him to say he was joking.

Tony wouldn't. When they realized he wasn't kidding, they glanced at each other and then back at Tony and Bill. They leaned back and started whispering together for almost a minute, which ended up being one of the longest minutes in Tony's life. He didn't want to lose them as clients, but he knew something was wrong with the deal and he really did want them to get the correct deal. He just couldn't figure out where these new figures had come from.

"One night. I promise. I'll get it done."

They stopped their whispering and looked at Tony, then looked at each other one more time.

Finally, the representative leaned forward and said, "This isn't the most professional way to go about it. But we understand this is a delicate matter. We'll give you one day. One! This is certainly an inconvenience, considering the other projects we have going on. Have it ready tomorrow. Otherwise, it will be weeks, maybe even a month, before we can return to finalize the deal."

The two men stood up and were on their way. After they'd left and were out of sight, Bill turned to Tony and asked, "Tony, why did you do that? We've gone over everything in that contract with a fine-toothed comb. What on earth did you see that was that bad?"

Tony pointed out the error to Bill "I don't remember that being in there when we were going over this."

"Really? That's it? Tony, their rep called me and told me about a new stipulation they needed in the deal and I changed the figure. Everything is fine."

Flummoxed, Tony stared back at Bill.

"The next time something like this comes up, talk to me before you make a promise like that. Did you notice how they both leaned back and had a private conversation amongst themselves? That's how you handle an audible like that. You don't just go off making an executive decision without talking to your partner first."

Bill let out a loud sigh. He was disappointed in Tony for the first time, but he'd known Tony would stumble eventually. No one is perfect. He decided it wasn't that big of a deal. If there was a mistake for Tony to make, he was glad the one he made was just postponing the deal instead of ruining it. So he stood up and, as calmly as he could, said, "It's okay. Mistakes happen. Just come back tomorrow ready to close, okay?" He put his hand on Tony's shoulder, smiled and walked into his office.

Tony stayed in his office for a while after everyone left, looking over the contract again. He could see what Bill was talking about, so he decided to take the rest of the day off and learn from his mistakes, do what Bill said and come back tomorrow ready to get the deal done. He drove around the city for a while and decided to go to the theater and watch a movie until Eva got off work. It was a movie he had wanted to see for a long time. He figured it would be the best way to get his mind off his recent blunder.

He was right. He felt a lot better as the day went on. He just kept telling himself that Bill didn't think it was a big mistake, so he shouldn't either.

When Eva got home from work, Tony was already home. He was doing a little tidying around the house when she came in.

"Hey, honey, how are you feeling?"

Eva set her purse down on the living room couch. She plopped down, let out a big sigh, and said, "Oh my God! I swear it was *don't listen to the teacher* day. The kids just didn't have any focus whatsoever. Neither class, at that. It's not like it was just one set of students--it was all of them. I felt bad for the two who actually came to school to learn, because they didn't have a chance. The other kids were just so disruptive. And whomever decided it was a bright idea to give phones to kids in middle school should be on trial for crimes against humanity!"

At this point, Tony had stopped moving and was listening intently. "Wow. I don't think I've ever heard you let loose like that."

"Well, I say all of that, but there were some moments that were pretty funny. You can't enjoy them, though. Teachers are not supposed to encourage negative behavior, funny or not."

"Yeah, I get that. Kids don't really know when to stop after you get them going."

"One of the kids hit another kid with a marker. I don't know how he got it, and I definitely sent him to the principal's office, but I wanted to laugh so bad," Eva said. She laughed at the occurrence now that she was home.

"Why?" Tony asked. "Well, for one, the other kid had it coming. Every time I looked up he was messing with the first kid. Kicking at his desk. Moving his papers every time he got up to sharpen his pencil. He was honestly being a pest. The problem is you can't really discipline them for that. As far as the school is concerned, that's just kids being kids. Now, Tony, I don't know how I knew to look up at this particular moment from grading papers, but I looked up and saw the other kid drawing back the marker. I should have said something then, but I thought to myself *no way will he actually do it*. The bully kid had gotten up to sharpen his pencil again and I can only imagine he had done something to annoy the poor first kid. So, he draws back, and I mean he looked like a professional quarterback. He hit the kid in stride, right in the eye," Eva said as she erupted in laughter. Of course I had to send him to the office, so I wrote his slip, got up, walked him out into the hallway and sent him to the principal's office."

"What do you think will happen to the little quarterback?" Tony asked as he chuckled alongside Eva.

"Honestly…not that much. The letter I wrote for him to take to the principal didn't mention the eye part."

"Really?! So you didn't want to rat him out?"

"Oh, I'll do you one better. When we got out into the hallway, I whispered *good shot* under my breath."

Now Tony was the one laughing out loud. "Really?"

"What?! The other kid had it coming."

"Oh my God. That's great. I wish I had a teacher like you when I was in school."

"Of course you do, I'm awesome," Eva said sarcastically.

"So what about you? How was your day?" Tony finally stopped laughing. "Eh, it was okay. Earlier I messed up this deal that we had for that big client I've been telling you about. But Bill kind of calmed me down and told me it wasn't such a huge mistake. I just have to learn from it and do better next time."

"How did you mess it up?"

"Nothing major. I saw some numbers in the contract that weren't there before. I thought I had made a mistake and punched in the wrong numbers, but apparently, they called Bill and asked for an amendment to the contract. Bill says it's okay, so tomorrow we're going to go in and finish the whole thing. See, no harm no foul."

"Don't you think he should have told you about the amendment *before* he just put in the contract and had you sign it?"

Tony stopped and thought about that for a second.

"I mean, that makes sense, but I trust Bill. He's been with me every step of the way. He wouldn't have made the change if he thought it was unreasonable. He's been a part of these negotiations just as much as I have, and he has just as much riding on it as I do."

"No, that's not what I'm saying. I'm saying--why not tell you? Don't you think it's odd given how closely you've been working on this deal together?"

Now Eva was fully upright and engaged. "I'm just saying, I'm not privy to how business works, but it just seems awfully strange to change something in a major deal so suddenly, right?"

"I mean, I get where you're coming from, but it's Bill. If it were anyone else, I would be nervous, but I trust Bill. He is a very integrous man. He wouldn't do anything illegal or anything."

Eva started reminiscing on what Tony's mother had said to her about looking out for Tony. Then she thought about the story she'd told her about Tony's father. She knew Tony was never interested in what had happened to his father. She was sure that was what he wanted everyone else to think. However, Eva knew better. She knew that more than likely, Tony just didn't want to hear it. He was afraid he might learn something he didn't want to know about his father.

But now, knowing what she knew, it was time for Tony to hear the truth. Eva knew he was headed down the same path as his father without even knowing it.

"Tony, I know it's a sensitive subject, but there's something you need to know."

"What's that?"

"I have to tell you what happened to your dad and how he lost his job when you were young."

"Wait, hold on. I didn't need to know it then and I don't need to know it now. Just…"

Eva interrupted. "Tony, listen. I know you look up to your father, but this is something I have to tell you."

"How do you even know what happened?"

"Your mother told me when we went to visit her the first time."

"Really?! You two hadn't even known each other a day, and she told you all of that?"

"I guess she had faith that we would make it. I don't know. But that's not what's important. She told me the story in case you were ever in a situation like this."

Tony fumed, but he knew Eva was adamant. She really believed this was something he absolutely needed to hear.

He decided to hear her out. "Okay, fine. Tell me what happened."

So, Eva proceeded to tell the tale of his father's fall from grace. Tony listened to her every word as he leaned forward on their couch, processing everything she said, a story he had avoided for so long. He couldn't believe what he heard. And he didn't know how to feel about it.

"You heard this straight from my mother?"

"Every word, more or less."

They both sat in silence as Tony sat and thought about everything Eva had said. He'd tried for so long to avoid hearing that story. Now he knew the truth.

"Eva…I know it was really hard for you to keep that secret from me. I can't say I'm happy I know what happened now. But I do understand why you had to tell me. So thank you. I know none of that was easy."

"I'm so sorry. I know you didn't want to hear it, but I'm glad you understand why I had to tell you. What will you do now?"

"Honestly…I don't know. That's a lot to consider. I do trust Bill, but I can't pretend like I might not have a real issue on my hands."

"Well, I'll tell you what. I'll go in the kitchen and make us a quick dinner and we can sleep on it."

Which they did. But they both knew there was an elephant in the room. Tomorrow, Tony would have a decision to make that only he could make. A decision which could change his life one way or the other. That night, he was up tossing and turning for most of the night, thinking about what he'd heard about his father.

When morning came, Tony was no closer to making his decision than he was when Eva had first told him. He woke up thinking about his father. He took a shower thinking about the story. He got dressed wondering what he should do.

Now he was on his way to work, still unsure about how he should handle the meeting. Finally, the time came. He was the first to the office. Bill had already laid out the contracts on the table. Tony stared at the one in front of his seat, completely in a trance, until Bill walked in with the two clients.

They all seemed to be overjoyed about something, as if yesterday never happened.

"Ah, Tony. I knew you'd be here. You're always on top of your game, aren't you?"

"I do my best, sir," Tony said as he cracked a smile. He didn't want to come off as nervous about the deal. While he was sitting there, he had decided he should trust Bill.

They all sat looking at one another for a moment and then Bill broke the silence. "Well, gentlemen, we all know why we're here. Let's get to it, shall we?"

Everyone took their respective pens and signed on the necessary lines. Page after page, Tony could almost feel the excitement permeate the room as all parties signed. He got back to the page that had held him up the last time and put his pen on the paper to sign.

Suddenly he remembered Eva's words.

She said they set your father up, Tony. Your father was a ruthless businessman. He was known for getting deals done by any means, as long as it was legal. Someone who wanted his position threatened his reputation and set him up to go on with a deal he shouldn't have. Tony, his people were embezzling money and found a way to put your father's name on the documents. Your father couldn't prove anything, so when he went to court, he signed a plea deal agreeing to settle it behind closed doors as long as your father admitted the wrongdoing. His lawyer told him they couldn't prove that he had nothing to do with it and advised him to sign. Your father's business practices put him on the bad side of a lot of people, so he didn't have a lot of people who would believe his story.

Tony reflected further on what Eva had told him last night.

Why is that popping into my head now? I can trust Bill. I know he wouldn't do anything like that to me. He could have picked anyone in this office. Why not pick someone who wasn't as productive as me if he was looking for someone to take the fall for something?

Tony kept trying to rationalize with himself, but something didn't feel right to him. He put the pen back on the paper again, ready to sign…but the pen didn't move.

"What's wrong, Tony?" Bill asked. He had glanced over and noticed Tony had stopped signing.

"I…I can't do it."

With raised eyebrows, Bill stopped and glared at Tony. "What do you mean, you can't do it?"

"I'm sorry, gentlemen," Tony said to the representatives across the table. He closed his contract and put the pen down. "The numbers in here aren't right and I can't do it. Something is off about this contract."

"TONY! Calm down, son. Everything is fine, I assure you!"

"I'm sorry. I know you are very busy men, but we need to find out where the new numbers in this deal are coming from."

Now Bill was starting to panic, anticipating this would offend his new clients. They all stared at each other, only for a few seconds, but those seconds felt like minutes. The clients then stood up, buttoned their suits and said, "We'll be in touch."

Then they left. Bill sat on at the table with his face in his hands. He should have been furious, but there he sat, not saying a word.

Tony sat down, turned his chair to face Bill, and said, "I'm sorry, Bill, but a long time ago my fath…"

"You're fired."

Chapter 11

Tony's posture stiffened in shock. "Wait, what? Why?"

Still sitting, now with his chin on his thumbs and his hands clasped, Bill said, "I know who your father is, Tony. After that lunch we had the day I visited your office, I knew your name sounded familiar, so I had a background check done on you. When I figured out who you were, and who he was to you, I had a great deal of respect for you. What happened to your father was terrible. I didn't know him personally, but I knew people at his company from my grunt days. To have people in your own company gunning for you like they did isn't new. The way they went about it, though, was criminal, in the most literal sense. I thought, to have this kid know what had happened to his father and still come back to this city and face those demons…to try to change his family's name and make his own legacy…that takes guts. I knew someone with those kinds of guts could thrive with the right leadership and coaching.

"Tony, I told you those numbers were legit. They were changed because they found someone in their company embezzling money, just like the people who set up your father, and they took swift legal action to get rid of and prosecute the guilty party. What you saw were the numbers that were sent back to them because of an auditing violation, which led to them catching their man in the first place. Their business can only thrive if they have a sterling reputation, and one employee put the entire company at risk. They were embarrassed. I'm sorry, but when the board catches wind of what happened here today, they'll call for your job. It's best that you just get a head start on it now so you can do what you need to do for your family's sake."

As Bill got up and walked out of the room, Tony found himself once again alone, sitting at the table and wondering what he had done.

How could something so good go so bad in 24 hours?

There would be no answers.

What was he supposed to do now?

How was he going to find another job as good as the one he had just thrown away? What was he supposed to think in this kind of situation? Was there anything he could have done different, besides just trust Bill like he'd thought he should in the first place?

"Wait. How am I going to tell Eva?"

Tony berated himself as shame filled his heart. He'd never thought he would be put in the same situation as his father had been when he had done so much in his personal and professional life to avoid it. Eventually, he stood up, made his way to his car and drove home.

As he sat waiting for Eva, the same questions persisted. He just knew he had done everything right. There was no way he could have been privy to the same information as Bill without Bill, himself, telling him.

So then why do I feel like such a monumental failure?

That night when Eva got home, Tony told her what had happened that day. How Bill had fired him. How he had thrown a golden opportunity down the drain because of a secret Bill had kept from him, as well as everything he had shared with Tony about what he knew about his father.

Tony was caught in a bad place. He believed in self-improvement and accountability, but he just couldn't see any wrongdoing on his part. Just before Eva had gotten home, he'd started to think…

If he had just told me what was going on…I'm smart enough to understand a simple audit violation, and if Bill knew my father had gone through this same thing…I mean…It's not like I would have thought it was beyond the realm of possibility. What more could I have done? I was completely honest and truthful with him with my concerns. Why couldn't he have given me the same respect?

Tony began to wonder if he was the one to blame for everything that had happened to him. Eva would do her best to be there for Tony. She reassured him that this was just a minor setback. That with his work experience and his considerable college transcript, he was young enough to find another career and work his way up and still be the man he wanted to be.

Eva herself, however, had her own internal struggle. She couldn't help but blame herself for the decision Tony had made that day.

If I'd never told him that story, he wouldn't even have thought twice about trusting Bill. He was right to trust him. But what choice did I have? It didn't sit right with him, either, and he could have ended up just like his father. What was I supposed to do? Was I wrong, too?

As Eva did her best to console Tony, deep down she knew she needed someone to console her. To tell her she wasn't wrong. That she had made the right choice.

For now, she decided, *I need to be here for Tony.*

That night, they mostly sat in silence. They didn't watch a movie or share in funny conversation. Neither of them knew what to say to the other. Tony knew he had to find a way to earn money as quickly as possible, but he didn't want Eva to be worried. Eva, in her heart, felt responsible for Tony's recent downfall.

Days passed. Brittany had since called all her friends and apologized for her recent behavior. She didn't know which ones were so concerned about her, but as far as she was concerned, they all deserved an apology for the person she had been over recent years.

After she had made the calls, she started examining other areas of her life. Things that led to her walking down the path she'd had in the first place. Places where she would ordinarily take her more resistant clients for fun and drinks were now off limits. She'd also decided she should no longer associate with people who only knew her in that domain. By all accounts, she decided, and was determined to follow through with, a complete life overhaul.

However, one problem remained. She still had a company to run, but her success had come primarily from her relationship with Jesse, with whom she had also called and broke off her arrangement. She'd let him know he might not care about his wife, but he certainly cared about his money. That if he tried to contact her again, she would let all of his clients know about their affair and how he didn't always hire the best people for the job. How he cut corners when it was convenient for him. Initially, he tried to resist and resurface his original threat. Little did he know the worst that could happen had already taken place. Eventually, he decided their arrangement was becoming more trouble than it was worth and hung up the phone.

She eventually got back to work. When she got back to her office, she called the board together and let them know she wanted to go in a different direction as a company.

"What do you mean?" one of them asked.

"I want this company to regain the reputation it had with my predecessor," she explained. "My father was right. Doing business the right way may not achieve the highest dollar amount, but it takes far less of a toll on a company. It allows us to lay a greater foundation. One misstep now and we could lose everything. That's largely due to the way I personally have gone about gaining and securing clients. For that, I apologize. I put this entire company at risk just to try to prove I was as good as my father. If this is agreeable, I would like to start the process of laying a greater foundation for this company on which to stand and rebuild."

The board looked around at each other and then back at Brittany. Now all eyes were on her as she anxiously waited for their response. Her heart beat faster as she spoke, and now even more so with anticipation.

Finally, they nodded. The head chair looked back at Brittany and said, "I think I speak for everyone when I say…we're pleased to meet you, Brittany."

Brittany's eyes widened in amazement.

"Now, how do you think we should go about this new plan of yours?"

Brittany almost began to cry. She hadn't known if the board would be lenient in wake of her show of contrition. She hadn't known if they would be accepting of her new direction for the company.

She composed herself and said, "Thank you all. That really means a lot. I was thinking about it last night and I believe we should start with the companies who were willing to business with us in good faith. I think in the past we did an amazing job with the work we performed and they might be willing to give us more referrals to widen our customer base."

"Okay, that's one way of going about it. I think you might be on to something."

Brittany and the board worked longer than usual that day. Brittany's new outlook had inspired the rest of the room to pursue her new vision. They brainstormed ideas for hours, creating new action plans and figuring out how to best service new clients when the referrals started coming in. By all accounts, it was one of the most productive work days in Brittany's career. It was certainly the one of which she was the most proud. Not for the production itself, but because she'd done it the way that it should be done. No tricks, no ace up her sleeve. It was just a good hard day of work, and she'd loved every second of it. She could see a great future for her company.

When she was done with the board, she decided to go into her office and get started figuring out who they could begin to contact the next day. She requested, and received, files on all the clients the company had done work for in recent years. As she looked over the files, she realized something. There was one glaring problem-- the list of people they had done business with in good faith wasn't that long. It was certainly much shorter than she'd thought it would be. She hadn't realized how much she'd depended on Jesse to bring her business.

She was worried. She glanced back and forth between the clock and the door as if Jesse was going to come back at any moment, but she knew that life was behind her. As she tried to force her nose back into her files, thoughts of Jesse and flashbacks of leaving to de-stress with one of her former paramours filled her mind. She soon realized that between her disappointment with what she had found thus far and the history she had with that office, she needed to change her scenery.

But she did not lose hope that she could find enough respectable clients. She decided to take the remaining files and boxes to her home. Once there, her head cleared of memories from the office and she returned to work, comping through her files with a fine-tooth comb. She looked at all the notes that were left for each and every file she picked up. To her relief, she found a good number of clients who were reputable and respectable.

However, it wasn't enough. The more files she picked up and put down, the more she found herself fidgeting anxiously between files. She remembered Blake walking out of their front door twice. The pain in his eyes she'd caused. She remembered having to tell him—again, twice--that she was having an affair. It was the hardest thing she had done in her entire life. Compared to having to look Blake in the eye and confess her darkest secret, running a company was tantamount to driving a smart car.

She winced at the thought as she looked away from the files, doubting she could find enough in her files for her to believe she could hit the ground running with her vision.

She stood up, walked to a window and gazed out.

Is this even worth it? Can I lead this company in this new direction? I knew it would be a process, but I didn't know we would be starting so far behind the eight-ball. Maybe I can call in other favors to increase our exposure. That won't solve the problem of my perception, though...

As she stood thinking of different ways to keep the company moving in the right direction, she had another epiphany.

Everywhere she got work done, whether it was the bar, her office or her home, there were memories of who she used to be. She realized the two main places she worked were unavoidable. It had to be done.

She had to go to the office to keep track of the progress of her new direction. Her office contained all of her important documents.

I mean…it is my company. I can just move my office. I don't have to have the best view in the company to still own it.

The solution seemed simple enough.

That left the issue of her home.

Is this place somewhere I could live and not feel as if I'm being crushed by a mountain? How can I stay here in the same place and forget everything I've done?

There were so many memories with Blake here. While there was a great deal of arguing and disagreements she provoked over the years, her memories weren't all bad. There were times she would come home and discover Blake had cooked for her. She loved the smell of his cooking. There were times when he had organized the files she had left on the living room coffee table while she'd gone out to the gym.

He really was a great guy.

She wondered if she would ever see him again, and if she did, what would she say? It wasn't as if the damage hadn't already been done. She could never take back what she'd done. She wished Blake would forgive her, but she also realized it might never happen.

And maybe it shouldn't happen.

She stared out the window, wondering if she would ever be able to return to the life she had built for herself before.

It was time for Tony's morning coffee with Jimmy. He, also, was feeling doubt. He didn't know if he could stomach telling Jimmy what he had done at work not even a week before. He had grown to respect Jimmy. More than respecting Jimmy as a person, he respected his mind. Jimmy had proven himself to be a very wise man in Tony's eyes. So when he sat down at the table and looked at Jimmy, he did so fearing what Jimmy might say to him. That was, if he chose to tell Jimmy about being fired.

"Tony! Hello sir. For a second there I didn't think you would make it."

"Oh, yeah. I'm sorry. I got out of the bed a little late this morning."

That immediately struck Jimmy as odd. "Got up a little late? You don't do *a little late*. Are you sick?"

Tony let out a long breath in anticipation. He didn't expect Jimmy to read too much into him being a little late. For a split second he thought about lying to Jimmy and just making up a story, but again, this was a man he respected. Even if he didn't want to tell Jimmy the truth, he also didn't want to lie to him and make Jimmy think any less of him.

"Well, actually, I got fired not too long ago. It's okay, though. I've already started looking for a new job. I'll land on my feet and be back to waking up early in no time," Tony said with a chuckle.

Jimmy, however, didn't share his appreciation for sarcasm in this instance. Instead he had a puzzled look on his face, as if he was looking for the answers to life on Tony's face.

"Well don't stop there. Why did you get fired?"

Tony proceeded to tell him about the two days leading up to his termination, everything from his first recognition of the new figures to his conversation with Eva. How he'd discovered what had led to his father's fate, as well as his conversation with Bill after the meeting. Jimmy just watched Tony intently the entire time, with the same expression of curiosity as he'd done when Tony had first told him he had lost his job.

Afterward, Jimmy glanced down at the table for a minute. Then he looked up and asked, "So why did you get fired?"

Now Tony was the one who looked puzzled, wondering if he was getting senile in his old age. Wondering why that would be Jimmy's question after everything he had heard.

"I just told you why I got fired. Along with the events leading up to said firing…"

"Well, you told me what happened. You didn't tell me why you got fired. So why did you get fired?"

Still confused, Tony said, "Because I botched a big win for my company over what turned out to be nothing. That's why I got fired."

"No--that's why he fired you. You still haven't answered my question, though. Why did you get fired?"

Now Tony was not just confused, but he clenched his teeth in irritation. For the first time since he'd met Jimmy, he started to feel anger toward the man. Not only did he not want to continue to talk about the worst failure of his life, but Jimmy just kept asking him the same odd question again and again.

"Okay, is this supposed to be some kind of joke? I'm telling you why I got fired and you keep asking me the same question."

However, if patience was a virtue, then Jimmy was the most virtuous man in that coffee shop. He had an abundance of patience and Tony wasn't about to break him, no matter how mad he was.

"If I'm still asking the same question then I must not have the answer yet."

"Or you're just not satisfied with the answer you're getting and you're just going to keep asking me the same question until I give you the answer that you like."

"If that were the case then why wouldn't I reword or manipulate the question to make the right words come out of your mouth?"

"Maybe because you get some primeval thrill out of it."

"Out of seeing you in pain? I assure you I do not."

Finally, Tony just gave in. "THEN I DON'T KNOW!"

Jimmy clasped his hands on the table and met Tony's gaze. Tony looked down and away, embarrassed that he'd just raised his voice at Jimmy. Finally, Jimmy broke the silence and said, "Tony--you are smart, punctual and hardworking. You're an ambitious man of character. You're meticulous in your work and you leave no stone unturned. When you're after something you become obsessed with it until you've done the best you can, am I right?"

Finally, Tony, glanced back up at Jimmy and said, "Yes sir."

Jimmy smiled. "So with all that being said, do you really think any employer would let you go just because you made one mistake?"

Tony's posture stiffened with amazement. Suddenly he understood what Jimmy was really trying to tell him.

"So, Tony. Why did you get fired?"

Tony paused for a few seconds before he finally said, "Because I let my past make my decision for me. Because I was so scared of ending up like my father that I didn't trust myself to make my own decisions," Tony said as he sank his face into his hands.

Jimmy smiled even bigger now. When he was listening to Tony tell his story, he'd had a feeling where Tony had gone wrong. When Tony got to the end about what Bill revealed to him, he was sure of it. But he knew there was still the task of helping Tony to realize it himself.

"It's okay, Tony. There's no need to feel bad about it. We all have something from which we're trying to escape. Many times we're so wrapped up in escaping what's behind us that we run into a brick wall in front of us. Some of us say ouch, get up, and find a way to break through the wall. Most of us feel that pain and, out of fear of the past catching up to us and our future putting up another brick wall for us to hit our head on, we end up curling into a ball and waiting there--just waiting for our future to fade away and our past to eat us alive. So don't curl up on me, Tony. You're too great of a man to let a little setback stop you."

Tony looked up at Jimmy and said, "Well, Jimmy, I really appreciate that. But the fact is, I will always be afraid of my past. What happened to my dad--it changed him. I never wanted to acknowledge it, but he just wasn't the same. It's like something died in him. Like he let the whole family down and it ate him alive. He couldn't shake it. That image will always be in my head, you know? I watched him torture himself for what happened, day after day. It's just not something you forget."

Jimmy let out one of his hearty laughs and said, "Well, who told you to forget it?"

Tony's eyes widened with surprise. "What? Why are you telling me all of this, then, if I'm supposed to carry that weight with me all of my life?"

"Who said it had to be baggage to tote around all of your life?"

Tony caught himself before he made the same mistake he had earlier. "Okay, so what are you saying?"

Jimmy took a deep breath and gave Tony a serious look. Tony noticed, and knew he had to listen very intently.

"Tony, what happened in your life is weight if you let it burden you. Your life is what you make it. Judging by the way you've worked to get to where you are despite your upbringing, I'm assuming you know that. So don't make that story weight, make it a lesson."

"A lesson?"

"Yes. A lesson. The most tragic stories in some of the best books ever written actually happened to someone. No one makes up those things out of thin air. Instead of letting those stories be a burden on their consciences, the authors put it in a book and decided to make them lessons for themselves and others."

"But how, though? I mean you're right, but still. That has to be tough to pull off."

"Right now you are an unstoppable force. Judging by what you told me about your father, with him being a ruthless businessman and all, I must assume he was too. What you need right now is immovable objects."

Tony interrupted with a laugh. "Hold on. You've lost me. Those are completely opposite things. That doesn't even make sense."

Jimmy replied, "You laugh, but I'm serious. Tell me, why do you think opposites can't coexist?"

"I don't know, but I'm assuming I'm wrong."

Jimmy laughed again and said, "You, and at one point your father, were bent on rising to the top. Nothing could stop you. Not fatigue, not competition and definitely not external naysayers. The same could be said of your father's descent. He just kept going further and further down and no one could save him from falling. He was an unstoppable force going down as much as he was going up."

Then Jimmy grabbed some containers on the table and formed them into a half circle. "But what if, when you hit something immovable, let's say something you can't control, like being fired. Instead of hitting the immovable object, racing downward and continuing to head that way unless something bounces you back up like, let's say, the lottery, on your way down you had a set of immovable objects. We'll call these *principles*.

"Wait. So how are *principles* immovable objects?"

"There are some things in life that are universal, but for some reason, they affect people in different ways. Have you ever been offered liquor before and not wanted it?"

Tony had a flashback to his college days with Jeremy and said, "You have no idea."

"Right. You're not an alcoholic but you're offered alcohol. Has a woman ever hit on you knowing you were in a relationship?"

"Unfortunately, yes."

"And I'd be willing to bet you didn't take her up on her offer."

"Of course not."

"So now, let's take two recovering alcoholics. Do you think they are never offered alcohol, even if by mistake?"

"Odds are, they are. Where is this going, exactly?" Tony asked as his curiosity grew.

"Just hang in there. I'm getting to my point. So--why do some alcoholics backslide while some never touch a bottle again in their lives? Why do some men and women sleep around on their significant others?"

The lightbulb went off in Tony's head all over again. "Immovable objects."

Jimmy tilted his head as he looked at Tony and said, "You didn't even let me get to the good part! But yes, because for them, the notion of not drinking or not sleeping outside of their bedroom is an immovable object. They don't even give it a second thought."

"That makes a lot of sense, but that's kind of extreme, don't you think?"

"Absolutely, it is! Listen--I'm not recommending everyone do it. People who don't know what direction they want to go in don't need immovable objects. I'm saying when you know what you want and you know what your purpose is, some things should be immovable."

Then Jimmy began to trace an imaginary line in the same shape as his half circle. "When you get knocked in the opposite direction, you have immovable objects to redirect you. You run into a commitment to your sobriety program, a commitment to be open with your sponsor, a commitment to never sleep with anyone other than your wife so long as you're married. Some principle that tells you to draw the line as soon as someone else starts to cross it and pull you into infidelity, and before you know it you're out of the presence of alcohol or someone trying to entice you away from someone with whom you've decided to spend the rest of your life.

"But again, the only way that works is if those things are immovable."

Tony understood what Jimmy was saying, but he was still unclear on how this applied to him. "How can I have immovable objects about something that happened at any job, though?"

Jimmy met Tony's eyes and smiled even bigger than before. He could see the light coming on inside of Tony and his high level of curiosity filled Jimmy with nostalgia.

"The objects aren't for the job, they're for you. Decide without question that failure isn't final, that you'll always get up one more time than you're knocked down, that there's nothing you can't accomplish if you really set your mind to it. When you've resolved that those things won't move, no matter how hard you're knocked down, you'll always end up redirected and going in the right direction."

"Even when someone else is in the wrong?"

Jimmy paused for a second. He wasn't sure if Tony was talking about his boss or if this was something else Tony had chosen not to divulge. However, he saw that Tony was listening intently for his answer.

"Tony, they say that a boy becomes a man when he puts away childish things. A part of being a child is an extreme level of narcissism, along with an incorrect feeling that the world revolves around you and what you want. I don't know what you're referring to, exactly, but I will tell you this. The main reason why good people get hurt more often than their less-virtuous counterparts is they are overly-accountable."

"How can someone be overly-accountable? If you did it then you did it and you need to take responsibility for it."

"And that is why I like you, son," Jimmy quickly retorted. "Yes. If YOU did it then YOU need to take responsibility for it. The problem is, most good people think accountability is the same as responsibility. A caretaker is held responsible for her patients. But if her patients die of natural causes, no one holds that caretaker accountable for their deaths."

"Tony, I want you to hear me well. Because Lord knows I don't want you go down this path. So often one might say, 'If I stop bugging them so much, they'll stop drinking,' or, 'If I change my body they'll be more attracted to me.' These are people who are holding themselves accountable for someone else's actions. Could you not bring up someone's biggest mistake on a daily basis? Yes. Could you take better care of yourself instead of looking sideways at people who do? Yes. But Tony, I don't believe demons are too keen on long-distance torment. Those demons don't come from far away. They are born within."

Tony was taken back again. He had never thought of what Jimmy was saying to be the case in most people.

"Someone may very well do you wrong. Here's the kicker…it has nothing to do with you."

"Wait. If I'm the one getting done wrong then it has to do with me."

"There's that kid again. Yes, you may be the unfortunate bystander, but it has nothing to do with you. If you don't believe me, next time you find someone doing wrong toward you or anyone else, walk away and see if it stops without them making a personal decision ***inside***."

"Ah, okay. I get what you're saying. That still doesn't answer my question, though. What does that have to do with my immovable objects?"

"Gosh, son, if you would listen, I told you to take your eyes off yourself. Your principles stay the same. You don't let anyone else's decisions be your responsibility. Somewhere there is a husband or wife crying right now, wishing they could change someone or something, when what they should be doing is helping the other one. They might be going through a fight in which they really need help. But they're too afraid to ask for help, or they're afraid of how they've been viewed. Maybe they don't even know what it's like to have someone love them unconditionally. Remember the *if/then* relationships? They may not even trust anyone enough to let them in. Take your eyes off yourself, Tony. That's the only way you'll be able to do a shred of good in this world."

Tony sat in a zone once again, trying to process everything his mentor had just shared with him. It was a very tall order. Tony still didn't quite understand it, but he got the main idea. He suddenly found himself suddenly rethinking a lot of things, one of which was his relationship with Jeremy. He wondered if he'd handled the situation correctly.

After what Jimmy had just shared, he decided to reconsider his former stance.

"Jimmy…thank you."

The two men got up and continued talking as they walked to the door. When they got to the door, Jimmy's phone started to ring.

"Go ahead, Tony. I need to take this."

Tony nodded and thanked Jimmy again. When Tony was out of the door, Jimmy picked up his phone. "Hello? Yes, I'm sure…"

Chapter 12

A week later, Brittany found a Café out of her usual way. She had grown tired of trying to work at home, knowing that she kept looking at the door waiting for Blake to open it. Instead, she'd decided to go to a new venue to think and get her work done. She'd started going places where she had never taken a client, nor had she been with Blake.

It was working. She noticed she was able to focus a little better and stay with the task at hand. As she was writing up new terms to add to their bids moving forward to ensure they gave the clients their trust and would give them a good reason to refer them for more projects, she had a new problem at hand. Since her time at her apartment a week ago, from time-to-time she'd been wondering if she should sell her company.

She was proud of the progress she had made with her new initiative. It was going better than she'd expected given the lack of clients she'd had good-faith negotiations with in the past. The problem was, she still couldn't escape the history she had in her office. No matter where her office was, she still had history in that building. From her meetings in secret with Jesse to her secret routes to go see a new lover. It was all in that building.

Finally, she let out a big sigh and looked up from her papers and…there was Blake, staring right at her. She froze. He was a few tables away, but those few tables might as well have been the length of a diesel truck.

She stood up slowly, hoping it wouldn't prompt him to walk away. She tiptoed over to him, wondering what she could say to him. He stood and they stared silently at each other.

Finally Blake said, "Yes?"

"Blake. Can we talk?"

"The last time we talked, it didn't go so well."

"I know. Blake, I am so sorry for the person I was. I know it's asking a lot for you even to look at me right now. Inside I feel like saying if you still have any love in your heart for me then you should sit down and give me another chance."

Brittany dropped her head as she tried to fight back tears. After a moment, she lifted her head and said, "But all I will say is I love you and I understand if you never want to see me again. I also know I would really love to sit down and talk to you."

Blake stared back at Brittany, wondering whether or not he should. Brittany was hurt, but what she didn't know was that Blake had cried just as much as she'd done when they'd last spoke. He'd sat in his car and blamed himself for everything that had happened with Brittany. Wondering why he hadn't seen it before. Wondering if there was something he could have done differently. Could he have helped her deal with her mother's loss better than she had? For weeks, he'd wondered what he could have done differently, until eventually he'd just decided shutting himself off was the only way he would ever get Brittany out of his mind.

But now, standing here looking at her again, he knew he still loved her, too.

"Okay, we can talk, but only for a little while. I have an appointment I have to keep."

As they sat down, they both gazed across at each other, feeling a sense of nostalgia. Neither spoke.

Brittany finally broke the silence and said, "I've missed you."

She waited for Blake to respond. Realizing he wouldn't, she continued. "I know you probably hate me. I can't say I blame you. If it's any consolation, I'm not the same person that I was. I've been actively trying to move my life in a different direction. That's why I'm here. When I'm at home I…"

Blake interrupted Brittany mid-sentence. "Do you still think about them?"

Brittany was taken off-guard. "What?"

"It's a simple question. Do you still think about the other guys you were sleeping with?"

Brittany sat quietly for a few seconds, wondering whether or not she should tell the truth. Lying and hiding things was what had gotten her in the mess she was in, but she knew that Blake would be mad if he knew that she did. She had a choice to make.

"Yes. I do."

Blake stood up and began to walk away before Brittany said, "Blake. Please sit back down. I can't handle you walking away from me right now. Just hear me out, please."

Blake stood with his back to Brittany, wondering if he should turn around. He knew this was the last chance for their relationship. He also wondered if he even wanted to be in this relationship anymore. It had brought him to his lowest moment through no fault of his own. He knew deep down that he still cared about Brittany. That part he could not deny. He decided to turn around and let her finish.

"Fine… what else do you have to say?"

Brittany was so happy that he'd turned back around that she almost forgot what she was going to say.

"I don't think about them in the way you're thinking. I think about them because when I'm at home I can't even get a glass of water without looking at the door, hoping you'll walk through it. When I do, I just think about what I did to you all over again and how I hurt you. The horrible things I did that made you walk out of the door in the first place. I can't go to our coffee shop around the corner without thinking about you. I can't sit down at our favorite restaurant without thinking about you. And every time I think about you walking out the door again, it's like my past is wrenching the happiness out of me like water out of a rag. The happiness we once shared."

"Yeah, I just didn't know the happiness was an illusion you'd created with lies and misdirection."

Brittany paused for a second and said, "I deserved that. But I've since changed my venues. I've apologized to everyone I could think of. I even apologized to the board at my company. I scrapped the past business partners who only did business with us due to my misdeeds. Only above-the-table deals are acceptable now, and the board members all know it and they're on board."

Blake was shocked. He moved closer to the edge of his seat with anticipation. That job was something Brittany held near and dear. He knew if she was changing things up there, then something was up. But he wasn't yet willing to let Brittany think all was forgiven.

"But even all that wasn't enough. My office is filled with the same bad memories. It's a trigger…and it breaks my heart every time I think about that part of my life. That's why I think…I'm going to sell the company."

Blake's body jumped slightly at what Brittany had just said. Since they'd left college, all Brittany had wanted to do was be better than the dad who had abandoned her. It had been her life. He truly couldn't believe what he was hearing.

"Are you sure you want to do that? I know how important that company is to you."

"You're right. It is. But if it means I can't be the woman you married or better then I don't want it anymore. Blake, I want you more than I want that company. If it's between you and the company, then I choose you 100 times out of 100.

I can't erase what I did, but I can make sure it never happens again."

Now Blake found himself trying not to cry. He could see the girl who'd walked up to him in that cafeteria line all over again.

"You know, your friends have been telling me you'd changed. I didn't know it was to this extent, though."

Blake grabbed her hand and held it for the first time since they'd broken apart.

"Maybe that's because I didn't want to believe them. But I can see it now. I know we still have a lot to work on, but I'm willing to give it a try if you are."

Brittany gazed at him with joy.

When Blake finished talking, all she could manage to do was nod her head as she wiped a tear from her cheek.

Then Blake stood up, still clasping her hand, and said, "Let's go home."

Meanwhile, Tony had been at home for a while, thinking about everything Jimmy had told him. His eyes had been opened to a new way of thinking and he didn't know how to process it all, but he was determined not to run from the new challenge. He would figure out how to live a better life and become a great man. Not because of what happened to his father, but because that's what he wanted to be for his family.

When Eva came home, she had brought groceries and the mail through the door. Tony sitting on the couch startled her a bit. She still wasn't used to Tony being home so early.

"I'm going to need you to leave a sign on the door when you're home from now on."

Tony laughed, knowing he'd taken Eva off-guard. "It's okay. I'll be back to being an obsessive workaholic in no time."

"Oh, you stopped? I think we should have you checked."

"You're just full of jokes tonight, aren't you?" Eva laughed as she set the groceries on the floor and sorted through the mail. "Hey, here's one for you."

"Listen, Eva, I had another one of my talks with Jimmy. He made me realize a lot about myself, one of which was that I can't let fear of the unknown dictate my actions. That other people's opinions aren't always right. I feel as if we've proven that time and time again. But that's another story for another day."

Tony slid off the couch and pulled a box out of his pocket.

"Eva Johnson…"

Eva's hands shot to her face. She couldn't believe what Tony was doing. They had been together since they were in college and she'd always known Tony would propose when he was ready. She just hadn't expected it to be on a night when he found himself unemployed. It went against everything she knew about him.

"Will you marry me?"

Eva couldn't contain herself. "OH MY GOD, YES!!!"

Tony popped up off the floor as Eva rose from the couch and they were quickly in one another's embrace.

"Oh my God. We have to take pictures. We have to go out and celebrate!! Tony, we're engaged!"

Tony let out a laugh that could rival anything he'd ever heard from Jimmy. "Yes, I know. Okay, well, come on. Get ready! We can take the pictures and let our families know."

Eva had paused, just as excited as she could possibly be. She didn't know what she should do first. "Okay, let me go put these groceries in the fridge first and then we can go." She picked up all of the bags and skipped to the kitchen and out of Tony's sight.

Tony sat down on the couch and leaned back. He was as happy as he could be about the decision he had just made. The envelope Eva had given him when she got home caught his eye. He decided to open it before they left, just to pass the time while he was waiting for Eva.

"You should have seen your dad's face when I asked him if I had his blessing to ask you to marry me. I think he was as shocked as you!" Tony called to Eva as he laughed.

He picked up the envelope and noticed the name on the front. Jericho James. He wasn't familiar with that name. Then he flipped it over to the back and noticed a very nice seal on the envelope.

"Wow. This must be someone important. Maybe it's a job offer.

Tony opened the envelope. It was a letter.

Hello, Tony. It's your old friend. You know me as Jimmy, but my real name is Jericho. I could tell from the first time we met that you didn't remember who I was. We actually met a long time ago when you came by one of my shops to buy a ring for Brittany when you were just a young man.

Brittany and Blake made it safely back home. On the way there, Brittany told Blake all about the changes she'd made and the apologies she'd offered up to all of her friends. She told him all about the new direction the company was going in and how she knew it would be in good hands after she left. They shared a nice conversation for the first time in what seemed like ages.

When they finally opened the door to the house, Blake's eyes lit up again. He couldn't believe his eyes. He just stood in the doorway, unsure of whether or not he should even walk in.

"Did you do this?" he asked Brittany.

"Yes," she responded. "What's wrong?"

"You cleaned…a lot!"

Brittany playfully hit Blake on the arm.

"Well, I'm not saying you didn't clean before. I mean, if anything, you would clean, but you never had time to clean like this. Wow."

Brittany pushed him into their home and said, "Oh yeah, wise guy? If you're impressed with this, just wait until you see the bedroom."

Blake grinned and said, "Really? What's in the bedroom?"

Brittany smiled back at him and said, "I guess you have to come with me and find out."

The two giggled as they kissed each another. Brittany's arms trailed up and she wrapped them around the back of Blake's neck, while Blake picked her up and held her in his arms.

Suddenly, they heard a knock at the door.

At Tony's house, he immediately thought back to the nice man at the ring store. Jericho. His hand shot to his head in disbelief.

Is that why I was so drawn to him that night outside of the restaurant? That was Jericho?!?!

Tony thought back to how nice he'd been when he gave Tony the ring he would later give to Brittany. Now, as an adult, he also realized Jericho had given him that ring at a tremendous discount.

But why, though?

He continued reading the letter.

I hope you aren't too cross with me after not revealing to you all this time who I was.. Typically, as children age into adults, they change. The world beats on them and they lose the spark of goodness they had as a child. Imagine my surprise when I sat on that bench that night, when I would sit in the coffee shops and feel joy in my heart that the kid I'd helped to win his lady love never lost that goodness. You're still just as smart and headstrong as you were the day I met you. You reminded me of my own son who I'd lost so long ago. Tony, don't ever lose that good thing. Fight for it, defend it, but most of all, share it. Don't let the world dictate who you will be.

I'm writing you this letter because I will be taking a sabbatical from this life I've built for myself. Don't worry. I'm not going anywhere to live out my days and die. I will return eventually. But honestly, I've grown tired of my responsibilities, the daily grind which has kept my mind from wandering into despair on more than one occasion. Now I think I'm ready to slow down and reflect on my life. Which is why, Tony, I want you to run my business in my stead.

Don't worry. I wouldn't be giving you this responsibility if I didn't think you could handle it. Also, you do not have to accept. I have already left specific instructions to pass it to another should you not accept. But when I asked myself who I thought would not only be capable, but deserved an opportunity like this, your name kept coming up in my mind. Please consider the offer. I think you would be a great fit. Should you accept, I have instructions on the next page of the next steps you should take, along with a phone that will be presented to you on your first day. It is a direct line to me should you have any questions or concerns.

I'm proud of the man you have become, Tony. I know you will be great."

Then the letter ended.

Meanwhile, Blake asked Brittany, "Are you expecting anyone?"

"No, I swear." He gently let Brittany down and she went to answer the door.

"Hey sunshine."…

"Dad???"

"You didn't think I'd miss one of my P.I.'s lurking around me, did you?"

Tony heard Eva walking up behind him, turned around, and said, "I think Jimmy just made me the owner of a business."

Eva responded, "I'm pregnant…"

To be continued…

Thank you for reading this book. I hope that it inspired you to give a second chance to someone who may need it.

For future news and upcoming projects, you can find me here

Twitter: @makeit2022
Instagram: @makeit2022

McEntry is available
For appearances
And
speaking engagements.

E-mail him at
mcentryrd88@me.com

About the author:

McEntry Ray Dunbar II was raised in Old Boston Texas. He went to school in Maud Texas, and college at ETBU in Marshall Texas. Mac was inspired to write by his time spent living in Texas, Louisiana, and California. Growing up and meeting different people from different backgrounds he noticed the need for stories to be told. Stories that brought people together rather than dividing them. Nearly deterred by a surgery and a heart complication he never let go of his dream of one day opening a center. A place where children could get the best start in life that they could, and adults could come and learn to be the best versions of themselves. To give everyone the one thing that we all need, a chance. He currently lives in Texas with his wife. They're expecting their first child.

Made in the USA
Lexington, KY
05 June 2019